Palm Reading

Unlock the Secrets of Palmistry to Discover About You and Your Future

© Copyright 2021

The contents of this book may not be reproduced, duplicated or transmitted without direct written permission from the author.

Under no circumstances will any legal responsibility or blame be held against the publisher for any reparation, damages, or monetary loss due to the information herein, either directly or indirectly.

Legal Notice:

You cannot amend, distribute, sell, use, quote or paraphrase any part or the content within this book without the consent of the author.

Disclaimer Notice:

Please note the information contained within this document is for educational and entertainment purposes only. No warranties of any kind are expressed or implied. Readers acknowledge that the author is not engaging in the rendering of legal, financial, medical or professional advice. Please consult a licensed professional before attempting any techniques outlined in this book.

By reading this document, the reader agrees that under no circumstances are is the author responsible for any losses, direct or indirect, which are incurred as a result of the use of information contained within this document, including, but not limited to, errors, omissions, or inaccuracies.

Your Free Gift (only available for a limited time)

Thanks for getting this book! If you want to learn more about various spirituality topics, then join Mari Silva's community and get a free guided meditation MP3 for awakening your third eye. This guided meditation mp3 is designed to open and strengthen ones third eye so you can experience a higher state of consciousness. Simply visit the link below the image to get started.

https://spiritualityspot.com/meditation

Contents

INTRODUCTION 1
CHAPTER ONE: AN ABRIDGED HISTORY OF PALM READING 3
    Commonly Asked Questions About Palm Reading 10
CHAPTER TWO: COMMON MISCONCEPTIONS ABOUT PALMISTRY 14
    Benefits of Palm Reading 18
    Other Benefits of Palm Reading 21
CHAPTER THREE: RIGHT OR LEFT - WHICH HAND TO READ? 22
    Superstitions that Influence Hand Choices in Palm Reading 26
CHAPTER FOUR: READING HAND SIZE AND SHAPE 28
    Types of Hands 32
CHAPTER FIVE: TEXTURE AND COLOR 38
    Color 42
    Flexibility 48
CHAPTER SIX: READING FINGERNAILS 54
    Nail Colors 58
    Signs on the Nail 60
    Nail Quality 61
CHAPTER SEVEN: READING THE ELEMENTS - HAND SHAPE 69
    Air Hand 70
    Earth Hand 72

WATER HAND	75
FIRE HAND	77
CHAPTER EIGHT: READING THE FINGERS	**79**
READING THE THUMB	89
CHAPTER NINE: READING THE MOUNTS AND THE PLAINS	**91**
CHECKING YOUR HEALTH THROUGH THE MOUNTS	99
CHAPTER TEN: READING THE LINES	**101**
CONCLUSION	**116**
HERE'S ANOTHER BOOK BY MARI SILVA THAT YOU MIGHT LIKE	**117**
YOUR FREE GIFT (ONLY AVAILABLE FOR A LIMITED TIME)	**118**
REFERENCES	**119**

Introduction

If someone told you that all details of your life are hidden in your palms, you probably wouldn't believe them. But indeed, your palm can tell you more about yourself than you think! Every single line on your palm is interconnected to different aspects of your life. If you can learn to read your own palm, then you do not need to go to tarot readers, astrologers, or palm readers to discover more about yourself. Many people don't realize it, but everything about your palm is an opening to learn more about yourself. The basis of palm reading is to use the shape, size, texture, colors, and the length of your hand and fingers to achieve self-realization on a deeper level than you can comprehend.

Some believe that the practice of palm reading or palmistry is one that only a select few people with unique gifts can use. Due to this, many people go to professional palm readers to learn more about themselves. This is not entirely right because palm reading is a practice you can engage in by yourself.

Palm reading can be learned and used by anyone willing to put in the work. If you are willing, you can also use this knowledge to help and impact those around you. By learning and understanding the art of palm reading, you can gain access to confidential information about your life, relationships, career, and basically everything that influences who you are as a person and the life you live. Palm reading can reveal your career path to you, so you don't waste your time pursuing something different. You can also learn about your social and romantic relationships. From your health to your family background and personal traits, there is much to learn through your hands.

Naturally, there are several resources online that claim to teach people everything they need to know about the practice of palm reading. Still, most of these resources often end up being more theoretical than practical. This realization can be genuinely frustrating and disappointing for people who genuinely want to learn how to read their palms and access information about themselves. If you are reading this, you should count yourself lucky since you don't have to worry about wasting your money on materials that do nothing for you.

Palm Reading: Unlock the Secrets of Palmistry to Discover About You and Your Future is your ultimate guide to mastering the art of palm reading. This book breaks down everything you need to know about palm reading with simplified and straightforward language, from the basics to the advanced. It does not matter whether you are a beginner or someone already familiar with this practice; there is something for everyone in this book. The first chapter gives you a brief insight into the history of palm reading. You cannot understand the present if you don't learn about the past. Throughout the rest of the book, you will learn about basic and advanced palm reading techniques, including how you can read the hand size, lines, fingers, colors, mounts, etc. More importantly, you will also learn how to make sense of whatever you read in your palms. This book was written to be your one-stop-shop for palmistry, and that is precisely what you will find.

Let's get you started on your journey to mastering palm reading and discovering more about yourself and your future!

Chapter One: An Abridged History of Palm Reading

Palm reading, or palmistry as it is also called, is often dismissed as another of those parlor tricks that psychics use to trick unsuspicious people into giving them a couple of bills. Many people don't believe this practice is real in any sense. Some even believe that palm reading is a new practice recently introduced to the psychic world. None of these beliefs are true. A lot of these beliefs are founded on a lack of knowledge about palmistry. This, precisely, is why I want to begin this chapter by giving you a brief look into the history of palm reading.

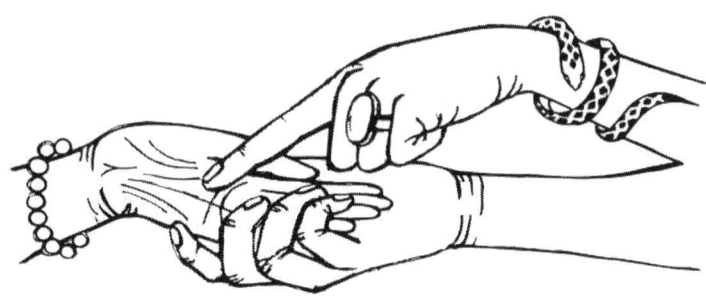

Palm reading, also called chiromancy or chirology, is the practice of reading a person's character and personality and predicting their future through the lines and undulations of their palms. To put it simply, palm reading entails foretelling a person's character and their future by reading the palm of their hands. It is not sure where palm reading originated from specifically. Palm reading experts don't agree on one place of origin, but what is certain is that palm reading has been around for centuries. Some believe that palm reading originated in ancient India and spread to other parts of the world. Knowing that the Roma gypsies once had their homes in India, this may be where they first learned the art of reading the palms. Regardless, palm reading has always been a widespread practice in China, Egypt, Tibet, Mesopotamia, and Persia. It was also popular in Ancient Greece, where it underwent significant developments. Briefly, let's talk about how palmistry spread from culture to culture.

According to Yoshiaki Omura, a renowned acupuncturist, palm reading has its roots in ancient Hindu astrology. This explains the relationship between palm reading and astrology, which you will learn about in a subsequent chapter. Millenia ago, the Hindu sage named Valmiki has produced a book on male palmistry with over 567 stanzas. The book's title means "The Teachings of Valmiki Maharshi on Male Palmistry." From India, palm reading traveled and spread to China, Tibet, Persia, and Egypt. From there, it spread to the European countries. The first place palmistry progressed was Ancient Greece. Some say that Anaxagoras, the pre-Socrates Greek philosopher, was an ardent practitioner of palmistry. According to reports, Aristotle, the philosopher, also found writing on the practice of palmistry on Hermes' altar. Aristotle reportedly presented his finding to Alexander the Great because he had a great interest in studying his officer's characters by examining and analyzing the lines on their hands' palms.

During the Renaissance Age, palmistry was regarded as one of the seven forbidden magic practices. The others are geomancy, necromancy, pyromancy, hydromancy, aeromancy, and scapulimancy. In the 16th century, the Catholic Church actively suppressed and fought the practice of palmistry. I should note that palmistry is referenced in one book in the Bible, specifically the Book of Job. Although this reference is indirect, it proves that palmistry has been around for thousands and thousands of years, contrary to what many people believe. The art of palmistry was soon revived in the 18th century, specifically in 1839, through the work of Captain Casimir Stanislas D'Arpentigny. This work was a publication titled <u>La Chirognomie</u>.

Katharine St. Hill later founded the Chirological Society of Great Britain in London in the year 1889. This society's objective was to procure advancements in palmistry and make palmistry a strategic art so much so charlatans couldn't abuse it. The Chirological Society's American branch was founded in 1897, eight years after the British branch was established.

One of the prominent figures in modern palmistry study was William John Warner, an Irishman usually called Cheiro. Warner studied and learned palmistry under Indian gurus, after which he established a palm-reading outfit in London. Cheiro became a very popular palmist. He had several quite high-profile clients, including the author Oscar Wilde. Cheiro's practice was pivotal in the spread of palmistry across Great Britain. Even people who didn't believe in occultism went to Cheiro to read their fortunes through their hands. In the following years, there were several attempts to establish a scientific foundation for the art of palm reading. In the 1900s, William G. Benham published The Laws of Scientific Reading for this very reason.

Despite the efforts made to suppress palm reading during the Middle Ages, the art has become one of the most popular occultic practices for divination. Palmistry is flourishing in this stressful modern age. Humans are relentless in their journey to search for answers and know the truth about themselves. One thing to know about palm reading's spread worldwide is that many original practice variations have developed in different cultures. This doesn't mean that the variations are watered down or less effective. The variations are mostly due to slight cultural differences. Having learned about palm reading's brief history, you must understand what palm reading entails in modern times.

Palm reading is a personal and ancient form of divination that reveals things within you and informs you of what you may expect in your future. Like any practice in esoterism and occultism, palm reading can be taught in different forms. It is also a very complicated practice, usually more complicated than other forms of readings or fortune-telling, such as tarot readings. Palm reading may be complicated, but this does not outrightly mean it is difficult or impossible to learn. It means that anyone who wants to learn this art must dedicate themselves to learning and understanding the practice's intricacies.

Reading a person's palm entails observing the lines and mounts of their hands and interpreting them based on their sizes, texture, quality, and intersections. In some variations of palm reading, a palmist (someone who practices palm reading) may also observe the fingers, fingerprints, fingernails, skin color, palm shape, skin patterns, and the hand's flexibility. Medical scientists and psychologists agree that the hands can reveal the truth about a person's health, character, and mental states. While palmistry is generally considered a science and an art, you are more likely to understand a person if you also have basic psychic abilities. Intuitive gifts such as clairvoyance make palm reading much easier for psychics.

Many people often wonder if palmistry is as accurate as other forms of psychic reading. You probably have this on your mind as well. It is difficult to say whether palm reading is more accurate than other forms of readings. The accuracy of palm reading depends on several factors. The first factor is the skill level of the palmist. When you practice palmistry, you cannot expect your readings to be as accurate as those of an experienced palmist practicing much longer than you. The more experienced you are, the higher your chances of getting an accurate reading. To become experienced, you need to put in many practice sessions and devote yourself to learning the art. Often, people learn palm reading to get it all in one go, but it does not work like that.

It may take months to get an accurate first reading. Now, getting one reading right differs from getting multiple readings right. To be consistent, you must practice often. Remember that palm reading is more of a learned skill than an innate ability one just possesses. You need to practice it as you would if you were just trying to learn a new language or a new musical instrument. The more you practice with yourself and other people, the more your reading accuracy will improve.

The second factor that determines palm reading accuracy is the age of the person getting a reading—your hands age alongside the rest of your body. In your younger years, the lines of your palms are as sharp as possible. You can see them clearly, so they are easier to read and interpret. But as you get older, the lines on your palm may blur with age. Some may also become more pronounced with age. Due to this, a palmist may find it challenging to get an accurate reading of your hand.

If you are a palmist, you may find it hard to read an older person's palms because of their age. Thankfully, some lines remain easy to read regardless of changes in age. Throughout a person's whole life, two main lines do not become difficult to read. You will discover more about these lines as you read on.

Accidents may also affect the accuracy of palm reading. Any accident that involves your hand may hinder your ability to read your own palms. Naturally, most people's hands often show signs of wear and tears. But if a person gets into an accident that results in burns or cuts in their hands, it becomes difficult to get accurate readings of their palms. Depending on the severity of the burns or cuts, readings may become difficult altogether. This means that people with significant scarring in their hands are unlikely to get palm reading. They must forego the possibility because the chances of getting accurate readings are arguably nonexistent.

Several other factors can affect palm readings' accuracy, but these are the three most significant reasons. To read your own palm or that of another person, you begin from the right hand. This is often the hand that most people use the most. Interestingly, some people argue that the right hand for reading is the dominant hand. Contextually, the dominant hand is whatever hand you regularly use to write, eat, and other activities. They believe that the dominant hand represents the conscious hand, while the other hand represents the subconscious. In some variations of palmistry, it is believed that the other hand contains information about hereditary traits or a person's past life. It depends on the beliefs of the palm reader. In palm reading, you must know the dominant hand before you start reading. Knowing whether a person is right-handed or left-handed will make all the difference in your reading. If you don't determine this before you begin your reading, you will probably end up with inaccurate results. The dominant hand reflects an individual's position on their essential inborn traits and attributes.

But the non-dominant hand gives you insight into the individual's family, parents, etc. By reading the non-dominant hand, you can ascertain which parent your subject takes after the most. More importantly, the information you find in a person's dominant hand is verifiable by what you find in their non-dominant hand. More likely, the dominant hand in most people is the right hand. But you should try to ask your subject about their dominant hand before you begin reading. Even when a person is versatile at using both of their hands, they often have one they utilize the most.

Your left hand is controlled and managed by your right brain, which is the part of your brain responsible for relationship understanding, pattern recognition, and other functions. The left hand represents your natural self, inner self, anima, and your lateral thinking ability. You may think of it as part of your personal and spiritual development. Your right hand is controlled and managed by the left hemisphere of your brain, which is in charge of language, logic, and reason. The left hand represents your objective self, outer self, education, social environment, and experiences. It also reflects linear thinking.

In palm reading, the right hand determines 80 percent of the reading, while the left-hand dictates the remaining 20 percent. Overall, a palmist focuses on reading the right hand and then adds or subtracts depending on the information they get from the left hand.

There is a scientific or systemic approach to palm reading that most people don't realize. To tell whether a palmist is real or a charlatan, you can do this by observing how they read the palm lines. As funny as this may sound, some palmists don't understand the science of palm reading. They just stare intensely at your palm and pretend to receive some revelation. Your hands form in the early gestation stages. Scientific researchers believe that the hands possess fossilized records of early human development. These records can be used to gain insight into what is yet to come.

Symmetry is one of the key things to observe in palm reading. Symmetrical hands in people can indicate athletic traits in people. If a man has symmetrical hands, it may mean he will have many children in his future. Abnormality in fingerprints is another thing that matters when taking a scientific approach to palm reading. According to researchers, men have more abnormal fingerprint patterns than women. This is usually because of their vulnerability to their environment. Suppose a man has an abnormality in their fingerprint patterns. There, it may indicate underlying health conditions such as diabetes or schizophrenia. Sweaty fingers in people indicate they are likely to be food addicts.

The bottom line here is that you have to be systemic in your approach to palm reading if you want to be more than just another palm reader. Many people already believe that palm reading is not real or authentic. To convince skeptics, you have to let them understand that palmistry is both a science and art by combining both approaches to improve your accuracy level.

Before I move on to the next chapter, below are some of the most frequently asked questions about palm reading and their answers.

Commonly Asked Questions About Palm Reading

It is natural to be curious. As a matter of fact, you require curiosity to be an accurate palm reader. The purpose of curiosity is to help you get answers, which is highly important. Understandably, there are lots of questions surrounding palm reading and practice. Unless you actually understand palm reading and what it entails, it will be difficult to practice yourself or the surrounding people. So, to aid your understanding of palm reading and how it can help you unlock hidden knowledge about yourself and your future, here are detailed answers to five of the most commonly asked questions about palmistry.

1. Is Palmistry a New Psychic Gift?

First, palm reading is one of the oldest psychic practices in history. It has been around for thousands of years, and it isn't going anywhere. Second, I like to tell people that palm reading is a skill anybody can hone, rather than a psychic gift that only a few possess. When people hear something like "gift," they automatically assume that it is an ability possessed by a select few.

Contrary to what we were made to believe through movies and shows while growing up, psychic gifts don't belong to a handful of "special" people. Every human has latent psychic skills that can be awakened through understanding and consistent practice. You need not pay a fortuneteller to reveal your future to you. You can become your own fortuneteller. While learning on your own can take a long time, it doesn't negate that you have that natural ability to hone whenever you feel like getting started.

2. Why are Palms so Important?

Everything about your palm is unique to just you, from your fingers to fingerprints. Your hands and palms are unique to you. Nobody else has the same fingers, palms, or hands as you. At a glance, our hands may all look. But when you take a more in-depth look, you can notice the slight changes in sizes, texture, colors, etc. Energy healers generally believe that one's hand is the extension of one's heart.

In retrospect, the heart is an extension of the soul and holds the secrets hidden deep in your soul. Basically, you can always tell whatever is in a person's heart by observing their hand (or palm). You can easily see that your hands are indeed an extension of your heart. You need your hands to touch, caress, express love, care, hug, and make love. You need your hands to give and receive. To hurt another person, you also need your hands. How you use your hands reflects the person you are deep within your soul and what you carry in your heart.

3. Is Palm Reading a Proven Science?

Palm reading didn't just originate out of nowhere in this modern day. It is a vast ancient practice that has survived thousands of years. So, you can tell it is more than just uninformed speculation like people assume. Over the years, modern authors have expanded on the knowledge of palm reading.

With the practice of palmistry, some palmists use a combination of psychology, astrology, superstition, and intuition, plus tiny bits of the original ancient palm reading knowledge. This discredits palmistry to many people. Even though intuition is accurate, sometimes it is not credible to make it all about palm reading. The reading itself is not the most important part of palmistry; interpretation is. Reading is one thing, and interpretation is another thing. Without proper understanding or knowledge, you can read correctly and then interpret inaccurately.

In answer to the question, palm reading is a science, but it is not yet a proven one backed by scientific research. But like I said, some studies in science have highlighted that the hand is truly a window to the soul, implying that palmistry is most likely an authentic practice. I like to compare the science of palmistry to Psychology. Even though there are founding principles on which palm reading operates, what matters the most is diagnosis and experience. Diagnosis is the reading, and with time, you become more experienced and versed at interpretation.

I should reiterate there is a scientific basis for palm reading. The number of nerves in your hands, which is outrageously enormous, is directly connected to your hands.

4. Is There a Connection Between Palm Reading and Astrology?

Contrary to what many people think, there is no connection between palmistry and astrology. If there is a connection, it is that both practices are used for fortune-telling and divination. Other than this, palmistry and astrology are two different streams of esoteric knowledge. But it is possible to combine readings from palmistry and astrology; this is up to the reader's discretion. Ancient palmists may have named the mounts of your hands after the planets, but this doesn't make astrology and palm reading intertwine. If you wish to combine both practices, that is your prerogative.

5. How Long Does Palm Reading Take?

The length of a palm reading session is subjective to the kind of reading you want. To explore yourself deeply, palm reading can take a long time. But suppose you just want information about your important qualities and traits or your destiny points. There, this reading may be brief and concise. How long your reading takes depends on what your intentions are and what you want to know.

These are five of the most common questions people ask about palmistry. In the next chapter, we will discuss common misconceptions about palmistry and the benefits of this practice.

Chapter Two: Common Misconceptions About Palmistry

Palmistry is one of the most famous psychic practices, which naturally means it is also one of the most misunderstood. The more popular and widespread, the more susceptible it is to misinterpretations and misconceptions. Thus, not surprisingly, palmistry is highly misunderstood, both as a science and an art. During the Renaissance, the suppression of the practice resulted in a culture of fear and skepticism around palm reading and other psychic phenomena. This created huge misconceptions around any topic in the psychic field and resulted in a deviation from palmistry's true purposes and processes.

To understand palmistry, you must get rid of any reservations you may have about it due to misconceptions and myths. Otherwise, you may not actualize your full palm reading potentials. How can you effectively practice something you don't honestly believe in?

One of the most common misconceptions about palm reading is the false belief that palmists are born with a supernatural gift. The media encourages this misconception through movies, TV shows, and other outlets. When you meet a palmist and see how easy it is for them to read and interpret your palms, you may think this is because they are born with that supernatural ability. You may not realize that they put hours into learning, studying, and practicing the skill. You don't just become a palm reader because you were born with the gift. You become a palm reader through dedication, patience, and consistency. Palmistry and clairvoyance are two skills that go hand-in-hand, and to develop these skills, you need to learn and practice. It is similar to how you learn how to fix the sink in your house.

Understandably, some people pick up the skills faster than others. But this does not mean they were born with magic or supernatural gift. It depends on how fast of a learner you are. Palmistry is more science-based than magical. If you are sharp at picking up details, you will do well at palm reading, no matter how subtle. Remember that the practice is based on observation. You don't need magic to become a great observer; you need practice. As long as you are willing to be patient in learning the different types of lines, mounts, line breaks, shapes, sizes, patterns, and other indicators connected to specific brain patterns, you will make a great palmist.

Another common misconception about palmistry is that it can predict death. This is entirely false and outrageous. Again, this is a misconception that was pushed and promoted by the media. Many people don't go for palm readings because they are scared they will come back with news or information about their death. Palmistry cannot predict when and how a person will die. The lifeline is wrongly considered the line that reveals the length of a person's life. Believing this, some palmists use it to predict when a person will supposedly die, justifying the fear many people already have about palm reading. The lifeline represents your level of passion for life, not how long you have left on earth. This will be discussed more in the chapter about lines.

Palmistry is also misinterpreted to be a practice that accurately predicts the future. Many people go to palm readers to expect that they will give them an in-depth, step-by-step prediction of what their future looks like. Palm readers cannot do this. A palm reader cannot tell you what you will have for breakfast tomorrow, but many people think they can or should be able to. Contrary to what many people think, the future is not predetermined. If the future isn't predetermined, anybody who tells you they can reveal what will happen to you in five years is a fraud.

The hands provide insight into the tendencies of your character and your personality, not your predetermined fate. You can infer projections about the future based on the pattern of behaviors you read on your hands. This is how palmists can make predictions about the future. Because behaviors can be changed, a palmist's "future" or projected outcome can also change. An experienced and empowering palm reader can help you change unhelpful patterns. This subsequently improves or changes the projected outcome of your future.

Generally, it is wrongly believed that a palmist should only read the dominant hand. Some also believe that only the right hand should be read. These are misconceptions that breed inaccuracy in readings. When you first begin reading palms, you will find that your right and left-hand lines are different. With the wrong information about the hand that should be read, it is easy for a beginner to lose interest in studying or practicing palmistry quickly. No one wants to continue learning a skill where they are not making any headway. There are two main misconceptions regarding the hand to use for readings.

The first misconception is that the left palm should be read for women, while the palm should be read for men. Some people believe this because the body's left side is for femininity and other related things. The right side concerns masculinity. This is true, but it does not affect the palm to use during a reading. Second, many believe that the hand one uses for writing should be used for palm reading. This is not true. The general agreement amongst palm reading experts is that the right hand, which is usually the dominant hand, should be used for reading since it is directly correlated to the logical brain. The hand connected to your brain's logical side reveals specific thoughts and behavioral patterns, which means it is suitable for readings.

One point of debate in palmistry is whether hand lines change or don't. Many people believe that hand lines don't change, which confuses beginners to palmistry. How can one get accurate readings if the hand lines are susceptible to changes? The answer to this goes back to palm reading's founding purpose, which many still misunderstand to date.

Palmistry is not precisely the art or science of revealing the future, as many like to believe. The original purpose of palmistry is to reveal patterns of behaviors and how they can change over time. The hand lines change according to changes in the brain; no one is born with a permanent set of lines – they change occasionally. Sometimes they become lighter, and at other times they become darker. If you pay attention to your lines, you might have noticed that they also change direction. For instance, if a person used to be high-strung, they can learn to become calmer and more levelheaded. When this happens, their hand lines may also shift in response to the behavioral pattern changes.

Also, many people think that palm reading is only about reading hand lines. This is a popular misconception, and some start palmistry believing it. The lines are not the only feature of your hand or palm. You can observe the hand in different ways. Palmists who know what they are doing will observe the length, shape, and texture of the fingers and the hand before they even go to the lines. They also observe more subtle features, such as the space between the fingers.

If you go to a palmist expecting them to give you information about when you will get married, you may leave disappointed. A palmist cannot tell you your marriage's timing by looking at your hand because that information isn't available there. What your hand can tell you is about your relationships. One can see strong or weak relationships. When palmists read about relationships, it does not necessarily have to be about romantic ones. Relationship readings can be about any close relationship. The belief that palm reading can reveal when and whom one is getting married is just another widespread myth.

Finally, palmistry cannot be learned in a few days or months. Expecting to learn or master the art of palm reading in just a few months is equal to setting yourself up for disappointment. This can take years to master. Practice is a critical component in mastering palm reading. So, don't set yourself up for failure by starting your lesson with the belief you will master how to read palms in a few months. Also, remember that palm reading is not paranormal. Thanks to the media, many people believe palm reading is paranormal. But really, it is just a study of the hands.

Debunking these common myths and misconceptions about palm reading is very important because it helps you and other new palmists understand what you are signing up for. Remember that understanding is the key to learning. You cannot learn unless you understand.

Benefits of Palm Reading

If palm reading cannot directly predict one's fortune, then what are the benefits? Well, you stand to gain a lot from learning the art of palm reading. Even though palm reading cannot tell you your destiny as it is set in stone, it can guide you on making changes that will affect your life in the best of ways. Palmistry links your past to your present to get insight into what you can expect in your future. The main benefit of palm reading is that it connects you with your dedicated, inner self. Your hand is the mirror of your soul. By learning to read your hand, you can open up a path to your soul to discover who you are and your purpose in life. An individual's task in life is to discover their purpose and fulfill that purpose. That is precisely what palm reading helps one achieve.

Palmistry is a means for you to journey deep within yourself and achieve true self-realization. More importantly, you also discover self-empowerment. You can address issues ranging from relationships to achieving your future goals and finding your spiritual path through palm reading.

Your life, like that of every other person on earth, is ever-changing. Life continually moves as we all endure the passage of time. Every moment in your life has been recorded on your palm. This is why five different lines represent different aspects of life, from love to work, reproduction, and life itself. Reading and interpreting these lines can reveal humongous information about your life, leading to true self-discovery.

It is often said nobody knows one better than oneself. This is true to some extent, but it is not the whole truth. You view yourself through a distorted lens. You may believe that you are a very charming and kind person, but if you look a little closer at yourself, you will undoubtedly find traits that cannot be described as charming.

You will discover things that contradict everything you believed you knew about yourself. Fortunately, your true self can be revealed through the palms of your hand. Through a palm reading, you can gain unbiased insight into your real personality. Friends may lie or distort the truth when you ask them what they think of you, but your hand would never hide the truth from you. A friend is unlikely to give you a hundred percent constructive criticism of your personality. Still, your hand can well do that. Your hand will tell you exactly who you are without overlooking any area of your personality, no matter how undesirable it may seem.

To know your strengths and weaknesses, palm reading can also help with this. Palmistry can help you gain insight into what motivates you and what holds you back. With an accurate reading, you can uncover your strengths and weaknesses and how they impact your life and the decisions you make. More importantly, you can identify your best qualities and determine how you can use them to improve your life.

Decisions are hard to make, especially when they are life-changing. But decision-making need not be hard. Whether you are thinking of quitting your job or moving in with a partner, palm reading can help you make the right decisions to steer your life towards the best path. By reading your palm, you can know the right direction to proceed in your relationships, career, and other areas of your life.

Palm reading won't spell the decision or solution out for you. Still, it will give you insight into what lies ahead of whatever path you want to choose. If you discover the path is the wrong one, you can easily change your decision and move on to the right path. When you know the right direction to follow, it means you are on the path to discovering your life's purpose. You can discover the perfect career path for you. Which field are you most likely to succeed in? This is one question you can get the answer to through palm reading.

Palmistry can help you understand why you are here on earth. Like everyone else, you have something to do on this earth. But not everyone knows what that purpose is. Unless you take active steps to discover your life's purpose, you may not realize what it is. Determining one's life purpose is one of the most challenging things to do as a human. It is hard to figure out what your destiny on earth is. Thankfully, a palm reading can be your key to knowing what that thing is.

Other Benefits of Palm Reading

• It can help uncover memories of past lives and how they relate to your present and future.

• Through palm reading, you can unleash your creative side and optimize your productivity and output.

• It can awaken your mind and set you on the path to spiritual awakening and enlightenment.

Palmistry can be used to address and solve issues in every aspect of life. Some things palm reading focuses on are the future goals of an individual and their choices regarding emotions. If you want an art that can help you with your career, relationships, finances, and other vital things, palmistry is the right choice!

Chapter Three: Right or Left - Which Hand to Read?

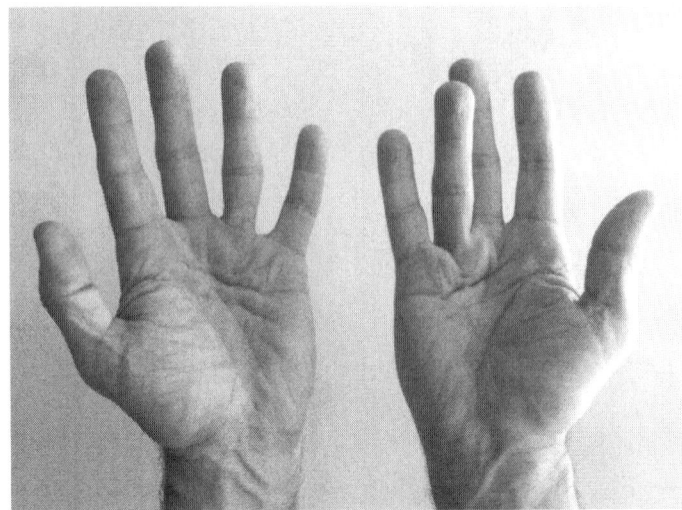

"Which hand do I read in palm reading?"

This is one of the most debated questions in palm reading. Although I have briefly explained this in the earlier chapter, discussing this more elaborately is vital to your understanding of palm reading. The hand is the single most crucial thing in palm reading. Without the hand, reading cannot take place. As important as the hand is in reading,

reading the right hand is even more critical. In this context, the right hand may refer to the right or left hand, depending on the palmistry variation a palm reader uses.

There is a sort of dissonance between the ancient and New Age forms of palm reading. They are both split on the hand to read and the one to exclude during palm reading. Some palm readers believe that the right hand should be read for men and the left hand for women. This is how reading is done in India, where the left hand represents the goddess Shiva and the right, Shiva's male consort, Shakti. In the Chinese variation of palmistry, though, it is the opposite. Chinese palmistry believes the right hand should be read for women (Yin) and men's left hand (Yang). This doesn't make the Indian technique more effective than the Chinese technique, or vice versa.

One thing generally agreed on is that the hand you use for reading makes a big difference in palmistry. Another thing that palmists generally agree on is that both hands should be used in a reading. So, as a palmist, never mistakenly read just one hand. It does not matter whether the hand you read is the right one to read - there will be inconsistencies in your reading. Any experienced palmist understands the essence of reading both the right and left hand and their reading differences. There are several differences in reading the right and left hands, based on the many palm-reading variations. Still, the only difference that matters is what they show to a palmist.

Overall, palmists agree that the hand you read in palmistry determines what is revealed to a palmist. This means that palm reading isn't about right vs. left hand. So the difference is based on hand dominance; you channel your energy through the hand you use the most. It is not advisable to make assumptions about the hand when doing a reading. For example, to do a reading on a friend, it is best to ask them for their dominant hand and their passive hand. The dominant hand represents a person's outer persona, which they reveal to friends, colleagues, and loved ones. Your outer world persona is whom the surrounding people interact with every day. The active hand gives insight into how you interact with the world and how the world perceives you.

But your passive hand represents your inner self – the part of you you only reveal to those that are closest to you. This is the side of you that comes to play when you are alone. It is whom you feel like when you are alone with yourself.

What if you use both your right and left hands equally?

This means you are ambidextrous. Ambidexters are harder to read for palmists. To determine which hand to read in an ambidextrous person, you have to check only their thumbs' strength in both hands; whichever hand has the more robust thumb is the dominant hand. Regardless of how one uses both hands skillfully, there will always be one more dominant than the other. Now, if you do your reading from the view of the left or right hand, both will give different insights. The left and right hand both focus on two versions of yourself: what you are and what you will/could be.

The left hand is often associated with what could/will be, rather than *what it is* presently. Your left hand can give insight into the opportunities you were born with. For example, if you read a person's left hand, you can tell whether they have a wealthy background. The left hand reveals information about the family, background, and opportunities a person is born with. It may also disclose information about a person's potential. Every human is born with potential, big or small, but only the right hand can reveal what is achievable with your potential, i.e., what you will be if you put that potential to work. So, the left hand only reveals what could be. The left hand can also provide insight into your personality and character. The passive hand can also do this, whether or not it is the left or right hand. Since the left hand is passive and less action-oriented in most people, it can expose your fears, quirks, and admirable qualities.

The right hand is the dominant hand in most people, which means it's used to engage in many daily life activities. This also means that the right hand carries the most action-based energy. In palmistry, the right hand reveals information about what you do with your potential. It tells you what you are. It can show you what you did to maximize your potential or where you fell short of that potential. Your right hand may also tell you your destiny or the likeliness of you fulfilling that destiny. It may also reveal your purpose to you. More importantly, your right hand can provide you with a broad scope of your present life, the actions you are taking, and how they can shape your future. This is what some misconceive as predicting the future.

Essentially, the most crucial thing in palm reading is to read both hands. Reading just one hand is akin to watching a movie halfway; you will never get to know the whole story or the outcome. By reading one hand exclusively, you are leaving out important information that can affect your interpretation. The best thing is to read both hands to get different details and consider when making your interpretation. For example, if you read your right hand exclusively, you might find you are about to experience a career change. Unless you read the other hand, you will not know the reason for the career change. If you read both hands, you might find that the career change resulted from a new opportunity you were privy to.

To put it more succinctly, a better understanding of who you are and who you could be is only achievable through dual-palm readings. By reading both your left and right or dominant and passive hand, you will understand your potential, where it can take you, and, More importantly, how you can utilize your potential to improve your life.

I should note there are cases where single-hand readings may be ideal. For example, if you just want a quick look into your personality traits, a single-hand reading can do that for you. You can get this information by reading only your left hand. You are unlikely to need a right-hand reading unless you want guidance on what personality changes to make. One more thing to note in reading is that you may change your reading styles depending on which hand you are reading.

Superstitions that Influence Hand Choices in Palm Reading

There used to be many superstitious beliefs about which hand to use in palm reading. Unfortunately, although most of these superstitions don't exist anymore, many traditional palmists still use them to determine which hand to read. Some palmists believe that hand choice in reading should be based on the gender of the person. Some believe that age is a determiner in the choice of hand for reading. Others believe that luck, accuracy, and line changes all play a determining role in which hand to read. Suppose you want to take the use of your palm reading knowledge beyond yourself. There, you must understand the reasoning behind these superstitions.

In the past, gender was often used to determine which hand to read, even though it makes no actual difference. Traditional palmists prefer to read women's left hand and men's right hand. Sometimes, they disregard reading the other hand, based on this belief. This belief was then because the right hand is the dominant and active hand in most people. Men used to be the ones with career and economic power, and as a result, palmists used to read their right hand.

On the contrary, women were more passive, with fewer career options and little to no economic power. So, traditional European palm readers disregarded reading a women's right hand. Instead, they focused on their left hand to discover more about their personality traits. As women's rights expanded, readers took a more egalitarian approach to palm reading. Still, some palmists stick to this technique regarding traditions.

Another belief that affected hand choice in palm reading is that the right hand should be read for people above 30, while the left hand is read for people under 30. This belief was because reading the right hand reveals what you become as an adult. Palmists then believed that reading the right hand for people under 30 would reveal too much information or, sometimes, divulge inaccurate information. Fortunately, this belief is not common among modern palmists because its validity has been disregarded over the years. You can find accomplishments and changes in the right hands of anybody, even children. There is no age-limit to accomplishments; hence, age shouldn't affect which hand you use for reading.

Traditional palmists used to believe that luck plays a part in hand choice for palm reading. The left hand used to be associated with bad luck. Actually, the word sinister originates from the Latin word for "left." Being left-handed used to be a form of stigma for many people in those days. If you were left-handed, you were automatically believed to carry bad luck. So, palmists often avoided reading the left hand because they don't want to spark lousy luck for themselves. Although this belief is almost nonexistent, many palmists still use it as an excuse to get out of reading both hands during a palm reading session.

The bottom line is that it does not matter which hand you read if you read both hands in a palmistry session. You cannot read one hand without the other. If you wish to unravel the truth about your life, you must read both hands. Reading each hand individually is the key to discovering their unique qualities. But dual-hand reading is crucial in interpreting what you learn separately from both hands to arrive at a wholesome outcome.

Now that you know which hand (or both) to use in palm reading, let's look at how to read hands based on size and shape.

Chapter Four: Reading Hand Size and Shape

The size and shape of your hands say more about you than you even know about yourself. Your hand size reveals a lot about your personality explicitly. If you are just starting in palm reading, hand size is one of the easiest things to learn and practice off the bat. This is why I am introducing you to actual reading with hand size. A person's hand size can either be small or large. But before I delve into what a small hand means and what large hands represent, you need to know what determines a large or small hand first. How do you know whether your hand is small or large?

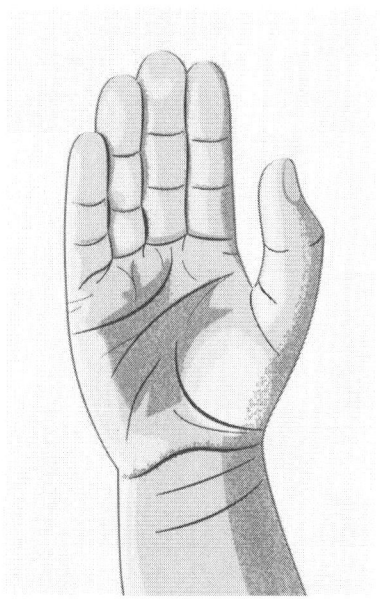

It is easy to make assumptions about small and large hands. At first, you may think that. When you consider that short people tend to have hands smaller than taller people, and adults generally have hands bigger than children, you will realize that the answer is not that simple or obvious. To determine your hand's size and whether it is small or large, you have to measure it relative to your body proportions. You cannot get your correct hand size if you measure it in relativity to other people. It doesn't matter whether your hand appears smaller beside that of another person.

One easy way to measure your hand size accurately is to hold your hand straight in front of your face, leaving the base of your palm to rest on your chin. Your fingers should be facing upward. Let the hand be straight, and try not to curve it around your nose. If your nose keeps you from holding your hand straight, leave some space between your hand and your face. If you have a large hand, you will find that your hand stretches beyond your forehead's middle point. The larger your hands, the more it stretches above the midpoint.

In contrast, a small hand reaches just below the middle point of your forehead. The smaller your hand, the farther it is from the midpoint. Suppose your hand reaches the midpoint of your forehead. There, this implies it is average-sized, and it likely combines qualities prominent in both small and large hands.

People's hands are relative to their body size. But there are people with disproportionate hand sizes. So, just because a person has a large body does not mean they have large hands. This goes for people with small bodies too. An individual can have a small body and somewhat large hands.

People with small hands tend to look at the bigger picture when making a decision. The smaller your hand, the more likely you are to consider the big picture when making any decision. Small hands mean you pay little attention to the tiny details; you focus on the critical details. This means you don't appreciate the details that may help break down a problem into smaller parts. Small-handed people try to solve a problem as a whole instead of doing it in parts. They are the definition of all-or-nothing.

Also, small-handed people tend to work in practical and creative fields. A small-handed person is more likely to be a sales manager than a large-handed person. They also delegate work to several people instead of participating in that process themselves. They want to see the progress of multiple endeavors at once, so they'd rather not be the one to deal with one problem in small, deep steps. This is because dealing with things on their own requires them to pay attention to the intricate details. As resourceful as small-handed people are, they prefer to work behind the scenes without seeking recognition for what they do.

Small-handed people may not like solving problems in steps and paying attention to the tiny details because they are prone to be quick-thinkers. Due to this, they like doing things fast and snappy. Solving a problem in steps while paying mind to the tiny details is a long process that takes quite a bit of time, and that is why small-handed people don't like to do this. This process is more suitable for people who take their time to solve a problem or address a need.

If you have small hands, then you are likely a quick decision-maker. You don't like to mull over things. You'd instead do it quickly and be done with it. This might make you act impulsively or take risks without analyzing all the details first. You may also prefer a busy life and complicated social situations where everything is fast-paced due to you being a quick thinker. You thrive best when things are busy and fast-paced.

The larger the hand of a person is, the more they like getting into all the details. Large-handed people find paying attention to details, no matter how small, enjoyable, and satisfactory. More importantly, they prefer to do things on their own rather than delegating to others. This attention to detail makes them notice problems faster than others. It also makes them more critical than small-handed people.

Regardless of gender, large-handed people tend to focus on one thing at a time. They cannot get involved in several processes simultaneously. To solve a problem, they carefully consider all the facts and figures before they arrive at a conclusion or use the outcome to decide. Because of their need to consider all the details, decision-making is a relatively lengthy and slow-paced process for them. Slow and steady is the best way to describe a large-handed person. The negative of paying attention to all the details is that a large-handed individual may get lost in the details. They often fail to see the bigger picture. Because of that fact, they need someone in their life who will regularly remind them of the bigger picture.

In palm reading, hand size is associated with the earth element. The larger your hands, the more earth element you have in your hand. As you will find in a later chapter, the earth element makes people steady and grounded. So, large-handed people tend to have those qualities that define steadiness. Even in social situations, they tend to be observant, patient, and thoughtful.

When doing a reading, you cannot make your conclusions by reading just the hand size. You need to consider the size in relation to the shape and other things such as the length of your fingers. It is common for palmists to see a small-handed person with other hand features that only make them potentially impulsive. Here, they may be less impulsive and more analytical in certain situations. For example, suppose you do a reading on a small-handed person. You get one sign that shows them to be impulsive and two other signs that imply they are cautious thinkers. This might mean they are generally cautious thinkers, but they often have moments of quick thinking and impulsiveness.

One of the most important things to consider when analyzing small or large hands is the hand's shape. The shape of the hand determines the kind of hand a person has. Below are the types of hand you will find when doing palm readings.

Types of Hands

Just as your face is unique to you, your hand is also unique to you. No two people have the same hands. Although hands may all look the same at first glance, you will find that people's hands are not identical. Still, to help you understand hands, experienced palmists have categorized the human hand into seven types. This helps for better classification and analysis when doing palm readings.

Note: In palmistry, hands are classified based on size, shape, elements, etc. The classification below is based on hand shapes. In a subsequent chapter, we will discuss the types of hands according to the elements. Remember that these things are intertwined. Below is a chart with illustrations of the type of hands.

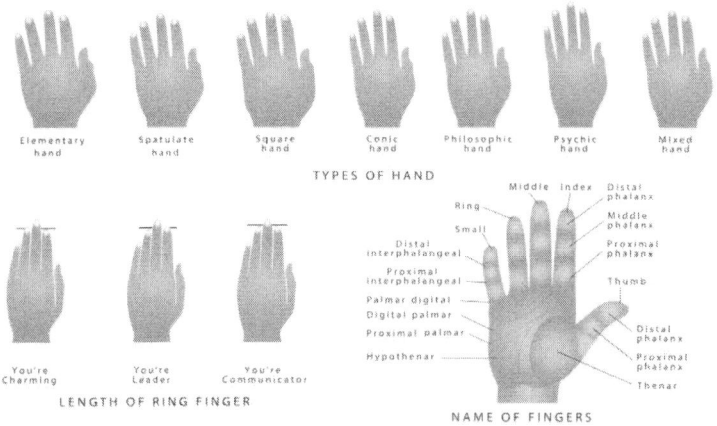

Elementary Hand

Elementary hands often have a thick texture, and the fingers appear to be short and stubby. This gives them a club-like appearance. The fingernails are usually broad, and the fingertips are somewhat squarish. The elementary hand is what you often find in people who fall under the labor class. This is the hand you see when doing a reading on a manual worker. The hand lines may be hard to read because they are lost in the coarseness of the hand. You may find it hard to spot distinctive lines, but they are usually short and straight when you see a line. Individuals like this tend to be hardworking and stubborn. Contrary to expectations, they often love their work because it genuinely makes them happy. Their hands reflect the years of hard work they have put in over their lifetime.

An individual with elementary hands may also have a pale hand color and coarse skin texture. Such a person may be temperamental, emotionless, unsympathetic, and slow thinking. They rarely think much of the future. Plus, they are pain-resistant more than any other hand. Note that elementary hands also have a tendency to be large. But sometimes, you might find a person with both small and elementary hands.

Square Hand

The square hand naturally appears to be a square. You can tell a square hand from the equal length of the palm and fingers. Sometimes, the base of the palm and the tips of the fingers appear almost equal. The thumbs are moderate-sized and well set. The nails of a square hand also look like a square, more or less. A person with square hands often has smaller hands compared to the rest of their body. The skin texture of a square hand is thick, rough, and coarse. Suppose you have square hands. There, you lead a convenient and realistic life. You also have a propensity for the smaller details when solving a problem or analyzing a condition.

A square-handed person is more likely to work in the business field than in any other field. They make very successful businessmen and businesswomen. This is mostly due to their social and outgoing disposition. But their tendency to be social and outgoing also makes them prone to volatility. If you have square hands, that means:

- You look at the practical side of things more often than not.
- You are not one to daydream about things. You would instead take action and get what you want to be done.
- You are more logical than emotional when making a decision.
- You are very strategic.
- You don't enjoy doing things in a hurry. You like to take your time.

Conic Hand

You may also refer to this type of hand as the artistic hand. From the name, you can tell that this hand appears to be a cone. The fingers of the conic hand are tapering. The texture of this hand is often soft and fleshy. Just because a person has artistic hands does not mean they are in the artistic field. Conic hands belong to people who are highly creative, imaginative, and artistic. Palmists call it the artistic hand because people with this hand tend to enjoy artistic things, such as paintings, drawings, colors, music, and nature.

A conic-handed person may be highly emotional, almost to the point of volatility. Also, they may be indolent and lazy. For a conic-handed person to achieve success and growth in life, it is crucial to keep laziness under control. Otherwise, it may become a stumbling block on their way to success. Conic-handed people often succeed as teachers, politicians, speakers, artists, etc.

But it is not advisable to make conclusions just by looking at the shape of the hand. When reading a conic hand, read the headline and observe the thumb in-depth to get a more resounding accuracy.

Spatulate Hand

The spatulate hand has an irregular shape and look. It often looks crooked with big pads in the fingertips. Another name for the spatulate hand is the active nervous hand. Generally, spatulate hands have massive fingertips. From the name, this hand looks somewhat like a spatula. Although the fingers are tapering like a conic hand, the palm's base is often broader. The thumb is also wide and large. The fingers' root is wider than the wrist, or the wrist is wider than the root of the fingers. It can go both ways. People with spatulate hands have an enormous amount of energy and strength. They can't keep their hands still because they frequently need to be channeling that energy towards something. This is one reason it is also called the active nervous hand.

If you have the spatulate hand, you love invention and discovery. You are innovative, and you put your imagination to work a lot. You also have a constant need for knowledge, so you may like reading books and searching for knowledge through other sources. Being spatulate-handed means you are excitable and restless by nature. This restlessness may also indicate enthusiasm towards achieving your goals. It also means you take risks without considering all possible angles. Due to the broader wrist, spatula hands mean you are impulsive. The broader finger roots represent practicality in everything you do.

If you have spatulate hands, you are likely to succeed in fields that require innovation and invention. You will make a great inventor, explorer, navigator, or engineer.

Philosophic Hand

Philosophic hands have a long, thin, and bony look, coupled with knotty joints. They often appear to be angular. A rule of thumb in palmistry is that people with philosophic hands are studious people. They have an excellent affinity for literature, and they consume books voraciously. A person with a philosophic hand would rather spend their time reading than spending time with friends.

For this reason, they may lead a lonely and ascetic life. Most people with philosophic hands enjoy sedentary work, which means they are usually involved with religious, spiritual, and philosophical activities. Those who contribute to science, philosophy, art, occultism, alchemy, and similar fields often possess philosophic hands. In this modern age, you can recognize such a person through their mechanical lifestyle.

To identify a philosophic hand, look out for a square-looking or angular base and knotty fingers. An individual with this kind of hand is efficient and driven by research. They have a thirst to know, so they often create new science, art, and literary theories. This is due to their studious and practical nature. One thing about the philosophic hand is it very rarely indicates material success. Also, people with philosophic hands have difficulty hoarding money, yet they may appear materialistic. Philosophic-handed people are mentally gifted.

Psychic Hand

This is also called the idealistic hand. Similar to the philosophic hand, the psychic hand is long and slender. But unlike the philosophic hand, the psychic hand often comes with smooth joints. The palm is thin and narrow, with a pale and smooth appearance. In this hand, you will find different lines along the surface. These lines signify the spiritual channels that a person will take along the way to their life path. The connection with spiritual energies and channels makes psychic-handed people idealistic. They don't concern themselves with material success and worldly achievements. They may appear to be less successful in life.

A psychic-handed person may take a more spiritual approach to issues because they are not thinking practically. But they also are imaginative, contemplative, and patient. Finally, they have high hopes for themselves, especially on spiritual matters.

Hand size and shape are pivotal in palm reading, but they are not the only things to look out for. Next, let's discuss hand texture and color and what they represent in reading and interpretation.

Chapter Five: Texture and Color

Many palmists go straight to hand lines during a palm reading session because they believe that is where the answer lies. But you can't get an accurate reading unless you take other things into perspective. Skin texture and palm color are two of the most essential things that can give you critical background information on a person's character, energy, and strength.

So, before you even proceed to the hand lines, you need to take an in-depth and critical look at the hand's texture, consistency, color, and flexibility. You can get a full understanding of a person's composition by noting these things. In more ways than one, these factors can influence your interpretation of what you read. For instance, there is a difference between how delicate skin and coarse skin affect health.

Texture is the first thing I want to explain in-depth because it affects the hand's color and consistency. Texture refers to the feel of the skin. When you touch your hand, how does it feel? Does it feel rough or smooth? The texture is your key to knowing your natural refinement. If your skin has a soft and delicate texture, that means you are a sensitive person. Everything you do is influenced by the quality of refinement of your skin texture. The quality of skin texture can estimate character and health. To determine texture, you have to rub your hand over the skin on the back of the hand.

- **Slightly Smooth**

Skin texture can be slightly smooth. This is a point between smoothness and coarseness. When someone has slightly smooth skin, it means that the texture is average. An average skin texture is often found in women. This skin texture is not so soft to where it feels silky. You can see relatively visible ridges when you look at the texture. More so, it feels like paper when you rub on it. Slightly smooth skin represents a moderate amount of sensitivity and energy. People with this skin type are usually receptive with fairly good conversational and social skills. You are likely to find this texture in doctors, lawyers, or an office worker.

- **Slightly Coarse**

Texture can also be slightly coarse, which means it tilts towards coarseness more than softness. A slightly coarse skin texture shows somewhat visible ridges on the palm and fingerprints. It is almost similar to the slightly smooth texture, but it feels a little coarser than paper. You will find this skin type in individuals who are physically and mentally vital to a reasonable extent. But they are neither particularly sensitive nor refined. People like this are motivated, hard-working, active, sporty, and well grounded.

- **Thin Skin**

Thin skin is another texture you will find in people. This skin type comes with more delicate lines than others. You will notice a fine line scattered all over with ridges almost invisible on the palm. The palm may appear to be transparent with veins and blotches showing. A person with thin skin is less vibrant because of a lack of sufficient physical energy. They also have increased physical and physiological sensitivity. They don't deal well with criticism. They also turn out to be impulsive and impatient.

- **Smooth and Delicate**

Smooth and delicate skin texture rarely has visible ridges and fingerprints. You can't easily pick out the ridges when reading a smooth and delicate hand. So, you have to be keen and observant to make sure you miss nothing. The palm of a smooth skin feels like silk to the touch. It is also covered in several fine lines. This is the most refined and sensitive skin. People with this skin type have a gentle, receptive, and introspective nature. They are often quiet because they would rather think about things than participate in gossip and needless talks.

- **Coarse Skin**

Coarse skin is also called rough skin. This is the skin type with hyper visible ridges. It often comes with significant lines on the palm. You are more likely to find this skin type on a man than a woman. When you touch this skin, don't be surprised it feels like sandpaper. Coarse skin is often abrasive and hardened to the touch. Rough-skinned people are less sensitive. They may not be sensitive. They often have a hard time with empathy.

Someone with rough skin may prefer to live an outdoor lifestyle. They would rather be out with nature than be stuck in closed spaces for long. They often find careers that involve hard work and manual labor, which is why you will mostly find this skin type in builders, farmers, and mechanics. If a person with rough skin isn't in the labor class, it can represent long-term stress.

- **Thick Skin**

Some palmists confuse thick skin and rough skin for each other. Some believe they are the same, but thick skin differs from rough skin. Unlike rough skin, thick skin comes with visible and deep lines. You can also see the ridges and fingerprints when you look at the skin. Note that thick skin can be coarse or smooth, depending on the person. But generally, thick-skinned people are healthy, energetic, and full of vitality. They are also less sensitive to criticism, but not in the same way as rough-skinned people.

- **Soft and Flabby**

Texture may also be soft and flabby. This is when the skin is loose. There is a discerning lack of firmness when you touch a skin like this. Usually, you find this texture in aging people. Otherwise, that means the person is indolent and daydreams or procrastinate. There is little evidence of muscular development in flabby skin, partly due to inactivity. Someone with this skin type may need to spend more time engaging in physical activities. Sometimes, loose and flabby skin is an indicator of ill health. It also indicates nervousness and sensitivity in some people.

Delicate skin portrays sensitivity and refinement. Delicate skin is often found in ambitious, goal-oriented, and practical people. But coarse skin portrays a lack of refinement or sensitivity. Coarse-skinned people are adventurous – yet noncompetitive. The thicker a person's skin, the more unrefined that person is. This lack of refinement comes with a lot of benefits. For example, rough-skinned people do not get nearly as ill as sensitive people because their skins protect their body from toxins. But when they do get sick, it comes down hard on them.

Color

Besides texture, color is also vital in palm reading. The color of your palm can tell the state of your health. By observing the palm of your hand, a professional palmist can discover any problems with your body and assess your physical condition. You can also use it to predict a set of patterns connected to your fate. Color can also be used to examine personality and character. To know someone's character, you can easily do this by studying his or her palm, precisely the color. Everyone has different palm colors. You may have pink palms while the person next to you has a yellow or red palm. Palm may also have a beige or white color. If you check your palm and that of another person simultaneously, you will observe a color difference. This difference may be subtle or vivid, depending on certain factors.

The color of your palm is your key to seeing how blood circulation goes on in your body. It also shows when there is a lack of circulation. Your blood runs through veins and arteries, and it absorbs and carries away impurities that can affect your life quality. In doing this, your blood is helping to renew and support your life. As the blood purifies your veins and arteries, your lungs also help purify your blood. Without the help of the heart, blood cannot run through the body continuously as it does.

Your skin gets its color from the quality and amount of blood flowing through your body. If the blood flowing through your body is impure, it shows on your skin and your palm. And it is often an indication that your health will suffer if you don't do something soon. Even if the blood is only half-pure, it affects the quality of your health, regardless. When the blood is flowing, it is evident from the skin. Should blood circulation become impure to the extent where it results in ill health, it can affect a person's mind and temperament. And this is how you can use palm color to know the state of a person's health, character, and behavioral pattern.

Before you do a reading, note that temperature could change the color of your palms. This is why the environment you do your reading in shouldn't be cold or hot. It should be just right. Also, when reading, observe the color of the palm, not the back of your hand. Color is less likely to change due to being outdoors or getting sunburned. The hand's thickness will also make a difference in your palm's color, which is why you must consider other features such as fingernails and palm lines.

White hands

White hands are pale-colored hands. They rarely show any sign of blood. Instead, they express a lack of warmth, coldness, desirability, and life. Pale-colored hands portray a lack of interest in social activities and pleasantries. They don't like to do things to please other people. The palm is white because the blood isn't circulating adequately. Maybe they have a weak heart, which makes it difficult for blood to pump effectively. White-handed people lack passion and enthusiasm. They are emotionally cold and have no interest in love.

But they are almost mystical. People like this also have a highly imaginative and active mind, which steers them towards literature. Health-wise, a white-handed person may be showing signs of anemia or some other dangerous blood disease. If both the palm and the fingers are pale and white, this may be a sign of hypertension. If the whiteness affects just the middle of the palm, it may mean the person is recently dealing with stomach trouble.

If someone has white hands:

- They lack enthusiasm for work or relationships
- They prefer to live alone
- They don't attend parties or social functions
- They deal with many financial problems
- They are mentally stressed

Sometimes, the white on the palm might appear bright instead of dull. Here, it means they are a little enthusiastic about their work. It also indicates a peaceful person.

Pink Hand

The pink hand indicates a healthy blood flow in the body, a sign of vitality and good health. Pink hand means that a person is warm, vibrant, and happy. They have just the right amount of blood pumping through their veins, so they do not feel pressured by overflow or weakened by an underflow. Pink may be light pink or dark pink. If someone's palm is dark pink, it means they can be made happy quickly. Generally, they experience and express emotions easily. They can also become angry quickly if they don't get what they want. Their thoughts are ever-changing. They may say something now and change their mind when the time comes.

Light-pink hands mean that a person is good-natured with happy thoughts. They are patient and peaceful. Happiness is a constant for them, and people admire them for their qualities. Regardless of their condition, they are always happy and grateful. They are always optimistic. They enjoy having people around them because they believe that is the key to enjoying life.

If someone has pink hands:

- They carry good luck around
- They often get double the amount of their input in anything
- They are physically and mentally vibrant
- They are surrounded by positive energy

The pink color is overall a sign of positivity all-round, from career to relationship to life as a whole.

Red Hand

If your palm is red, it indicates an intense blood flow. The redness of the palm is based on the force of the blood flow through the body. It shows a level of intensity applied to everything from business to love or social life. Someone with a red hand may have difficulty controlling his or her emotions. They lose their temper over the flimsiest issues. The lack of self-control can push them to the point of aggressiveness and even physical violence. But sometimes, it depends on where the redness is on your hand. If the redness is more prominent in the palm than any other place, this may mean they can't control their anger. Conversely, if the red is shiny and smooth, it indicates financial prosperity and auspiciousness.

If the redness only appears in some parts of the palm, it may indicate that a person has blood pressure problems. Deep red means that the person may soon suffer from a nerve-related health problem. They may also deal with high blood pressure and other related conditions. Red-handed people are usually hospitable. If the red is bright, it indicates that such a person likes to take a hands-on approach to solve problems and addressing their needs. This does not mean they don't trust or believe in other people. They just like to do things by themselves.

If someone has red hands:

- They are temperamental
- They have a problem with self-control
- They are often serious-minded and responsible
- They are prone to succeeding at things they do

Someone with a red hand needs to be careful of their temper because it makes them vulnerable to being hit by a stroke or falling ill to other conditions.

Blue or Purple Hand

The hand may be bluish or purplish looking because of inadequate blood flow. This usually means you are in poor health. Blue rarely affects temperament; it often indicates health. If your hands appear to be bluish, it may reveal a weak pulse in the heart. If the palm shows blue or purple all over, it is an indication of critical health. But if the blue only appears as spots on your palm, it means that blood flow is imbalanced in the body.

There, you are not in a critical state of health. Suppose you check someone's palm, and you get something that shows they might have health problems. There, it is best to advise them to see a doctor instead of outrightly telling them they likely have a heart problem or something else. This is to avoid frightening them.

If someone has blue hands:

- They are generally indifferent and introverted
- They may be prone to heart problems
- They need to pay more attention to their health
- They are dependent on others

Blue also suggests that a person is dealing with fear, likely irrational or not.

Yellow Hand

Yellowish palms can be a pointer to over-secretion of bile, which could lead to liver dysfunction. In the body, bile is crucial to the digestion of food. Typically, it shouldn't be found in the blood to the extent where you can see it on your skin. When bile somehow ends up in the bloodstream, the body perceives it as a foreign invader it must naturally get rid of. If it becomes too much in the bloodstream and eventually shows on the skin, it makes the palm assume a yellowish look. Excess bile in the bloodstream can irritate your brain and nerves. This might cause you to become cranky, moody, and cynical. Depending on how yellow your palm is, you might even become gloomy.

When you are easily irritated and unsociable, you don't make good company. This inadvertently affects your social life and possibly your relationships with loved ones. If the yellow color goes beyond the palm to your nails and hand lines, it could mean you are dealing with a more severe condition.

If an individual has yellow hands:

- They may be dealing with more than one disease
- They easily attract partners
- They need to check their diet and eating habit
- Their health requires more attention

Yellow hands may also indicate that they are unlucky with gambling and activities related to money.

Black or Muddy Hand

Some people have blackish or muddy hand color, which reflects a life of struggles. Black indicates negativity in health, career, and relationship. It may also be a pointer to the conflict in the future. A person with black hands may face many problems in life. They are prone to health and financial problems, as well as social isolation. Black hand is often taken as a sign of bad luck. If the blackness only appears as spots on the hand, this could be a sign of disease. Someone with this hand color should continuously find ways to improve their physical and overall condition. Otherwise, they may live their whole life, moving from one struggle to another.

Note: Colors are not permanent. Whatever color a person's hand shows at a specific time reflects their health and character then. Meaning, a person's color cannot always remain the same. Sometimes, palms change color due to inadequate blood circulation in the body. Other times, color changes occur because of some adverse event. It helps to pay attention to your palm and watch as the color changes. If you regularly pay mind to these changes, you can turn situations in your favor. The best color to have is pink color, which indicates good health, good character, and a quality state of mind.

I would like to note you should never outrightly diagnose a medical condition through palm reading. Whatever you get in your reading, always back it up by consulting with a licensed medical practitioner. Don't diagnose diseases just from palm color or texture alone. Remember, these indices are ever-changing depending on the person involved.

Flexibility

Flexibility refers to the ability of your hand to adapt itself to different conditions. The flexibility of your hand reflects the flexibility of your hand. It also shows the quality and overall condition of your mind. Basically, a flexible hand equals a flexible mind, and a stiff hand equals a stiff mind. Yet, it is not that simple. There are gray areas when examining the flexibility of your hand. When doing a hand analysis, flexibility is checked to evaluate the mental state of a person.

The flexibility of your hand is portrayed by how easily it bends backward. To examine your hand's flexibility, stretch your right hand outward with the palms looking upward. Then, use your left hand to exert pressure on the stretched hand until it bends as backward as possible. The farther your hand goes, the more flexible it is. When you do this simple exercise, observe whether your hand as a whole is flexible or if you can only bend it at the joint of your knuckles. If your whole hand is flexible, you will find that your fingers bend alongside your knuckle joints. During your examination, you may notice there are varying degrees of flexibility. The hand can stretch back up to 45 degrees. In someone else, it might bend to where it takes some time even to straighten your fingers. It depends on how flexible your mind and your emotions are.

Usually, there are three degrees of flexibility in the hand. First, you have the standard flexibility. Also called regular or average flexibility, when you press back on your hand, it opens wide and straight to its full extent. This kind of flexibility is considered good enough in palmistry. Second, some hands form a graceful arch when you bend them back, and it doesn't cause pain when you do this. This is considered very flexible. Then, you have the hands that don't open up no matter how you press them backward. Even if you want them to open to their full extent, they can because of the fingers' inability to extend. These are called *stiff hands* because they barely have any flexibility.

When you have average flexible hands, it means you find it easy to adapt to life. You are versatile in how you approach issues. If you have stiff hands, it implies that you don't appreciate change. You always want things to remain as they are. You may find it hard to change your habits or behaviors. It also means you don't particularly consider other people's perspectives on issues. You prefer to stick with your own view.

If your hand is what we call very flexible, that means you are very adaptable and versatile. But if you have hands like this, coupled with other features that also indicate versatility, this can pose a problem. You may become too versatile to the extent where you can't master one thing. Remember that saying, "Jack of all trades, master of none?" Well, that would be the perfect saying to describe you. The thumb you have may determine whether you can control your flexibility. We will refer to this in the chapter about thumbs.

Stiff Hand

People with stiff hands are typically unprogressive. They are rarely innovative because they prefer to stick to the traditional ways of doing things. They believe in working hard and saving to generate wealth. Stiff-handed people don't think success is achievable in any other way except through hard work, saving, and deprivation. So, you won't find them spending their money on the latest gadgets. Though, just as their hands are stiff, their mouths are also tightly closed. You can trust a stiff-handed person with your secret because they are unlikely to tell it to another person. This is partly due to their stinginess. Yes, they are stingy, even with information. Below are traits common with stiff hands:

- Closemindedness and immobility of the mind
- Overly cautious of new people and adventures
- Inclined to stinginess and narrowness
- Lack of adaptability
- Fear of adventures and new ideas
- Traditional

Average Flexible Hand

This is the hand of someone that likes to approach things moderately. They are balanced in everything they do. People with averagely flexible hands take life seriously. They are continually trying to understand life. They strive to understand the difficulties of the human race. As thoughtful, earnest, and broad-minded as they are, they are within bounds in their thinking. They defy extremism.

- A balanced sense of self-control
- Likes to remain within safe boundaries instead of pushing for the extreme
- Listens and understand before responding to issues
- Neither rash nor over-enthusiastic
- Ability to use and spend money properly
- Reasonably charitable and outgoing
- Sympathetic towards others
- Not held back by traditions

Very Flexible Hand

When the hand is flexible, it also means that the mind is highly mobile. It portrays someone who can quickly adapt to any situation, almost to the point of faultiness. The more flexible your mind is, the more brilliant you are. This shows in the characters of people with very flexible hands. They can do many things at once. Their talents are diverse, which makes them prone to an inability to focus in one direction. If you have a flexible hand, you are likely to be very generous, sympathetic, and empathetic. You don't believe money should be hoarded. You believe it should be used in securing your wants and possibly that of your close ones.

- Emotional and empathetic
- Quick-thinking and learning
- A tendency to overthink things
- Creative, imaginative, and artistic
- Extremely generous with money and resources
- Self-aware and introspective
- Ability to master and understand the impression of others

Hair on Hand

When you become very experienced in the art of palmistry, you will find you don't even need to see the person's face before you can decipher and reveal things about them. Suppose you have to read a person behind a curtain. This means you can't see their face. Here, the hair on that person's hand is important to your study. It helps to know about the rules around the growth of hair on the hand. The hair is one-way nature fulfills its purpose (s) in connection with our body.

Scientists say that hairs are similar to tubes that connect to your skin and nerves. The energy in your body exits through the hair. Thus, you can determine the nature of a person by examining and analyzing their hair color. Since energy exits through the hair, it affects the color of the hand. Basically, the hair color on your hand reflects the energy coursing through your whole system.

For example, if you have a considerable amount of iron in your system, it flows through the tubes and colors the hair. The color could be black, blond, brown, white, or even gray, depending on the amount of iron or pigment in your body. People with blond or fair-looking hair often have small amounts of iron and pigment in their system. As a rule of thumb, people like this are generally gentle, languid, and listless. They are also more susceptible to influences from their environment than people with darker hair.

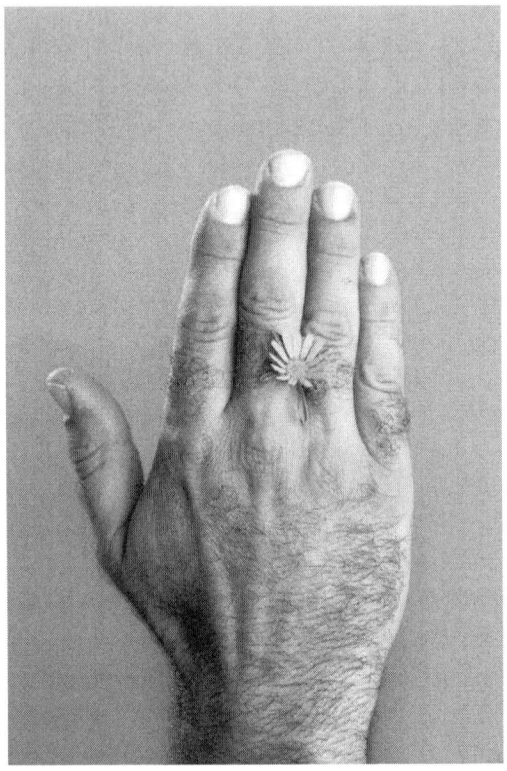

Individuals with dark hair tend to be passionate, temperamental, and less energetic when working. They are also highly irritable yet affectionate than people with fairer hair. Often, the color of the hair on the hand also determines its texture. For instance, red hair is usually coarser than other hair colors such as brown, blond, and black. The tubes through which energy passes to exit the hair may be wider depending on the amount of energy coursing through. It may make a person very excitable and impulsive if the energy is forceful and of great quantity.

When a person starts getting old, the energy generated considerably reduces. It also no longer emits through the hair tubes since most of it used to keep the body going. When this happens, it results in a decline of pigment flow through the hair. This makes the hair turn white, which is why a person's hair may become whiter the older they become. Other things that often result in white hair include shock and grief. How does this happen? When one experiences something that triggers grief or shock, there is a rush of nervous energy that forcefully flows through the hair tube with the pigments. The natural reaction to this is that the hair turns white. Rarely will the hair gain its color back after experiencing such a strain.

Let's take the United States, for example. Many people in the U.S. have white hair on their hands due to a mix of different factors. The first is the climatic conditions, which causes people to develop a competitive mindset. The state of mind of people in the U.S. typically keeps them on their feet. Despite circumstances, they don't mind enjoying life. Another factor that causes white hair is the kind of lifestyle pressure that many people experience. These factors and more can contribute to how hair color appear on people's hands.

Chapter Six: Reading Fingernails

Initially, I wanted to talk about the fingernails under the color and texture chapter, but I decided against it because the fingernail is one of the most critical components to study in hand analysis. It deserves to have its own chapter. The color, texture, and shape of your fingernail can say a great deal about you to someone who knows how to read fingernails.

In palm reading, you can tell an individual's luck by looking at their fingernail's shape. The size of the fingernail can also determine the character of a person. You can learn more about yourself by studying your fingernails. Just like skin texture, nails show the quality of different aspects of your life. It also reflects the health of your nervous system. The healthier your nervous system, the healthier your names will appear. Fingernails protect your nerve endings, so your ability to cope with stress is evident in their appearance. The longer and larger your nails, the more you can cope with stress. This also applies to the opposite. One by one, I discuss the meaning of the fingernail's color, shape, and size.

In most people, the nail shape is based on the type of fingertip, i.e., if the fingertip is narrow or thick. Before we delve into this, keep in mind that your nail can change over time, depending on your habits. For instance, someone who continually deals with stress, anger, or nervousness may develop a fan-shaped nail. But if the problem causing the stress or anger goes away, the nail returns to its natural shape. Small fingernails can become more prominent over time if a person changes their habit or lifestyle.

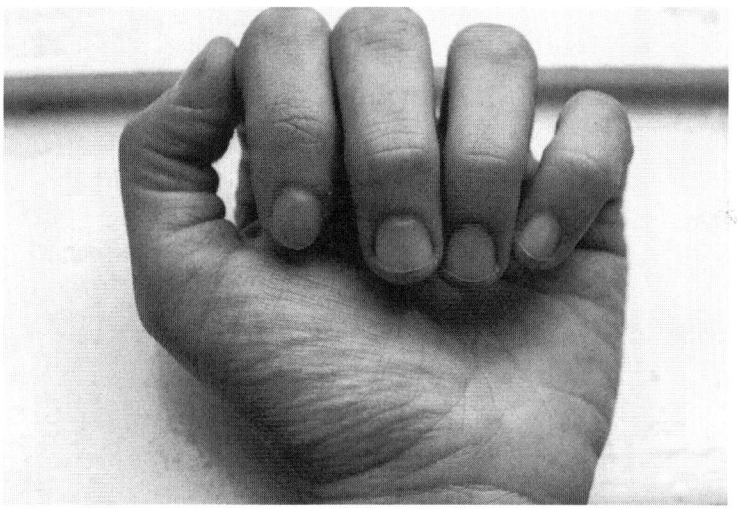

The shape of the fingernail is typically classified by length and width. Usually, the reasonable length a person's nails should be is half the upper phalange's length. Realistically, the nail should neither be short nor long. It shouldn't be bitten.

So, you have:

- **Large and Broad Nails**

    The wider a nail is, the healthier and stronger your nervous system is. Physiologically, people with large and broad nails have stamina, which means they are resilient. They can stay calm amid any situation, no matter how rousing the situation is. They are also very patient. The largeness of the nails makes the excellent shields for nerve endings. This keeps their nervous system in excellent shape, which in turn influences their ability to cope with stressful and triggering situations. If the nail is wide and short with a small space between the fingertip and the nail, it shows an individual who is critical and judgmental of others. Such a person is quick-tempered and quite opinionated. But if the nail is both broad and long, it portrays someone honest and straightforward.

- **Long and Narrow Nails**

Narrow fingernails suggest a sensitive nervous system. Sometimes, it indicates a lack of strength. People with this kind of nails are usually mild-tempered and romantic. Now, if the thin nails are long, it means you are also a very imaginative person. You are inclined to pay attention to your environment and your surroundings' details, which makes you very creative. But you also tend to believe and trust people easily. As a result, you need to work on increasing your alertness. This will help protect you from potential harm in your environment. Also, long and narrow nails may indicate that you have tough luck with interpersonal relationships. Your relationships rarely work out, and when they do, they don't last that long. Narrow and short nails portray someone selfish, materialistic, and narrow-minded. Such a person may also be afraid to take risks.

- **Small Nails**

Small fingernails are typically closer to the fingertips. They tend to be narrow, with plenty of flesh on both sides. If you have this type of nail, you likely have a curious nature. You love to know things, so you are always inquiring and seeking knowledge. You are also sharp, witty, and may find it challenging to manage your emotions. Small nails may also mean that your resistance to illness is low.

- **Short Nails**

Nails often become short due to years of biting. If the nail is short, to where it looks like half of a nail, it shows a critical person with an uneven temper. This person may also be argumentative, meaning they get into conflicts and debates. It does not matter whether the nail is broad or narrow. This characteristic is peculiar to people with short nails. If you have short nails, you may get bored quickly. You may also be hard to please. If your nails are only slightly short, that portrays a quizzical nature.

- **Oval/Round Nails**

This is the most general nail shape. It portrays someone with a well-rounded and balanced nature. Someone like this rarely responds to a situation with anger or spitefulness. If the round nail is long, it could mean that their health is not in good shape. A broad and round nail suggests an individual with a kind and gentle disposition. This means you can get along with everybody. Your social skill is at an admirable high. This person is also adaptable, versatile, and creative. If round and small, it suggests a lack of physical or mental strength.

- **Fan-Shaped Nails**

A fan-shaped nail is narrow at the base in comparison with the tip. Coupled with a soft skin texture, a fan-shaped nail suggests someone who constantly battles with nervousness, stress, illness, and a lack of vibrancy. On a firmer skin texture, though, this nail portrays someone sensitive and possibly bad-tempered, yet determined. Depending on which finger has the fan-shaped nail, the meaning can change from finger to finger. On the middle finger, a fan-shaped nail means you continuously worry over your business, career, or money. On the index finger, it shows someone that always stresses overachieving personal and professional goals. On your ring finger, it means you are struggling with artistic expression. On the pinkie, it gives information about intimacy and communication.

- **Rectangle-Shaped Nails**

A rectangle nail also relatively wide may indicate a thoughtful and conscious personality. This means you put deep thoughts into your decisions. You are a deep thinker by nature. You are also sympathetic, easy-going, and tolerant of others. If the rectangle nail is long, it may indicate a lack of diplomacy. A narrow rectangle nail shows you are unwilling to take risks, impatient, and narrow-minded.

- **Squarish Nails**

Finally, you have a square-shaped nail, which is the most robust nail type. It indicates vital and good health, plus an even temper. But if the nail is tiny and squarish, you may not be even-tempered. People with this nail type are reliable, serious-minded, practical, and upfront. They also are intelligent and good-natured.

Nail Colors

Nail colors are typically used to evaluate a person's hand. When using fingernail colors to look for health signs, you use the same principles as you do with the hand. The principle is to find something unusual in color combined with the nail quality. A nail with a delicate texture has shiny and smooth nails. If the hand is smooth, but the nails are rough looking, this means that something is out of balance. That may well be the subject's health. Coarse nails are usually found on large and rough-looking hands.

Typically, nails take up to six months to grow from the base to the tip. Some markings on a nail are timed based on their location at a point in time. For instance, if you find a horizontal ridge along with the nail, it suggests that a change occurred around two to three months ago. Pliability can be used to evaluate a healthy nail. A pliable nail is, on average, thick with a smooth texture and has a light pink color. The moons on pliable nails are typically milky white and visible on the thumb.

- **Bluish or Purplish Nail**

If you see a bluish or purplish tinge around the nail bed, it could indicate possible respiratory or circulatory issues. The appearance of this color may be due to weather, which means it is temporary. In early teenage and menopausal years, women often have bluish nails - this is absolutely normal. It indicates no health problems. Blue may appear on and off a person's nails due to changes in their hormones.

- **Whitish Nail**

A whitish color in the nail bed suggests iron deficiency, liver dysfunction, and low vitality. If the white is pale and greyish, it could indicate that a person lacks warmth. This could also mean that one is selfish. Depending on your nails' quality, this could also portray a fungal disease, especially if the nail is dry and brittle. If the full nail is white with a cloudy spot on the tip and a yellowish base, it may suggest potential kidney disease.

- **Yellow or Brown Nail**

Yellow or brown nails often mean the same thing. A brownish color in the nail bed may indicate a liver condition. It could also suggest a person has jaundice. If you have a high level of bilirubin in your bloodstream, it can also result in yellowish and brownish spots. Other conditions that may cause your nails to take on a yellow color include fungal infection.

- **Red Nail**

Red fingernails indicate poor blood circulation. If the nails are too red, it may be due to blood pressure problems or cardiovascular disease.

Signs on the Nail

Colored spots sometimes appear on the nails. The appearance of spots on the nails means different things in relation to the type of moons on the nails.

- **Black Spots:** If you have black spots on your nails, this could mean your blood is impure. As a result, you become vulnerable to diseases that are linked to blood impurity. This could be malaria, fever, typhoid, etc. Black spots often appear on the nails temporarily, after which they disappear. Luckwise, a black spot suggests someone prone to misfortune and calamity. If a black spot appears on a person's thumb, it may indicate they will commit a crime in the nearest future. On the index finger, a black spot may indicate the loss of a loved one. If it appears on the pinkie, it suggests a failure in achieving set goals.

- **White Spots**: Typically indicates an obstruction of blood flow and possible disease. If a white spot appears on your thumb, it could mean you will find love soon. It represents success in business if found on your index finger. A white spot on the middle finger could mean you will go on a journey soon. If you find a white spot on your Apollo finger, it indicates a potential rise in status or life as a whole. Finally, a white spot on the pinkie means you are close to achieving your aim in life. As I have said, you need to consider this information with other things before you make an interpretation.

•Half-Moon at the Root of Nails: This typically represents progress in life. On the index finger, it means you are up for a promotion at work or that you will hear some good news soon. Half-moon on the Saturn finger means you may be expecting some sort of monetary benefit. On the Apollo finger, it means a rise in your societal status. You are likely to become famous in society. This is a lucky sign. If you find a half-moon on your little finger, it portrays an unexpected success in business. On the thumb, a half-moon indicates the growth and success of all kinds. Sometimes, the moon sign becomes bigger than half. When this happens, it almost covers half of the nail, indicating that something negative will happen.

Some people don't have the half-moon (lunula) at the base of their fingernails. Usually, the lunula is ever-present on the base of the thumb. Its absence points to inadequate aerobic capacity and blood circulation. Also, it may be a sign of malnutrition or anemia.

Nail Quality

As you have learned, one can also get information about health through the quality of the nails. To evaluate the health of your fingernails, know what to look for. A healthy fingernail:

- Has a light pink color
- Curved nail plate when you face it towards your eyes
- Has a visible white half-moon at the base that becomes more visible when you push your cuticle.
- There are no permanent spots, ridges, grooves, indentations, or lines.

If your nails do not have at least three of these qualities, you can't be sure about the quality.

If nails appear to be sunken in, this is called a concave nail. This nail portrays physical stress and a general lack of energy. It could become softened due to overexposure to chemicals or water or due to a nutritional deficiency. A concave nail warns of an impending illness, which may be severe.

Humped nail is the direct opposite of the conclave nail. It is typically associated with respiratory disorders, such as pneumonia or emphysema. A humped nail may indicate a weak lung. Smokers have this kind of nail, which suggests inadequate oxygenation. A humped nail with a swollen and severely bitten appearance points to more severe conditions. Sometimes, nails grow over the fingertips and end up looking claw-like. This is common with people who have a dominant nature. People like this may also be problematic. Where someone has humped fingers and no respiratory problems, it signifies tenacity and arrogance.

When the nails are weak and brittle, it signifies a mineral imbalance, which may be due to a low diet. Sometimes, it points to an under-functioning thyroid gland. A person who regularly works in the garden or uses their bare hand for works that involve the use of chemicals is likely to have weak and brittle nails. Sometimes, weak nails are due to the skin's dryness on the hand, usually resulting from long-time stress.

Pitting

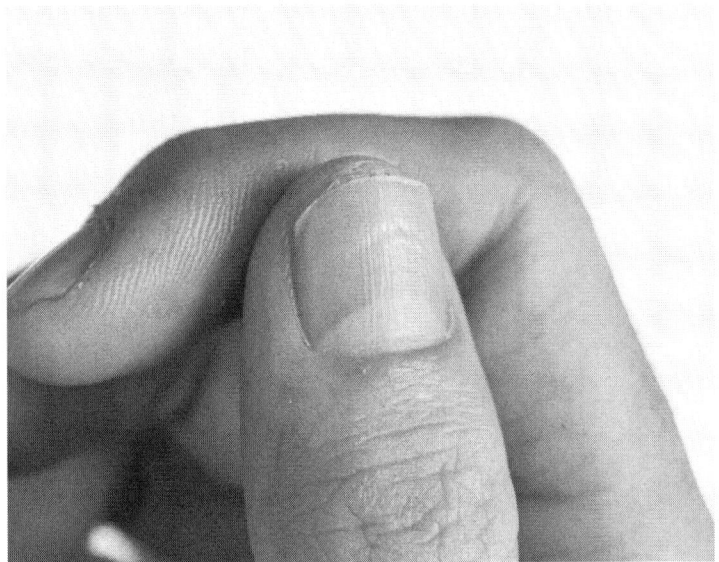

Fingernail pitting is when there are tiny holes all around your nail plate. When this happens, your nail may look somewhat like the moon's surface, except with tiny craters. Nail pitting often indicates the presence of one or more skin conditions. If the pits are scattered all over your fingernail plate, it could mean you are dealing with psoriasis. This causes the appearance of scaly patches on the skin. If the pits look like a grid, that may be alopecia areata, another skin condition that causes hair loss in small, round patches. Finger pitting could also suggest eczema nail injuries.

Ridges

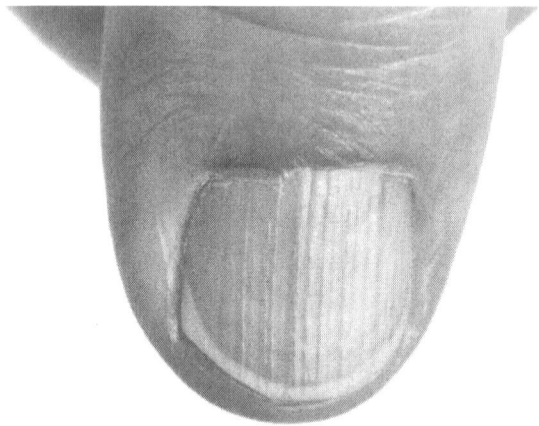

These are indentations that stretch from the base of the nail up to the tip. They may be vertical or horizontal. They are common indicators of stress and anxiety. If your nails have ridges that appear on all the fingers, it suggests an abrupt change in health, possibly due to stress, infection, dieting, or trauma. Vertical ridges often appear with old age. But, if you find them on a young adult, it represents hormonal changes, nervousness, or poor nutrition. Some people may have ridges on their nails due to the constant use of nail polishers. Should this happen, it could be a cause of nervousness or stress.

Beau's Lines

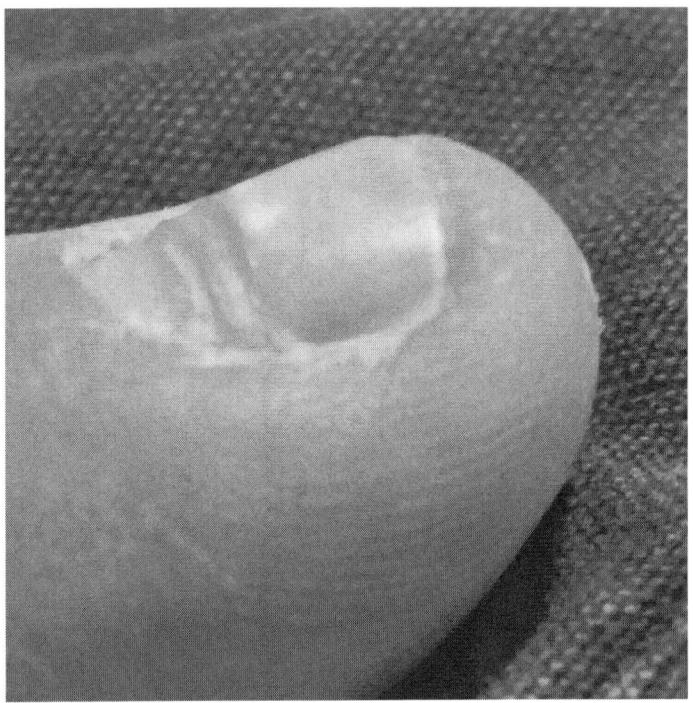

These have nothing to do with relationships. Beau's lines are named after Joseph Beau, who was the first to describe them and their meanings. Beau's lines are deep lines with a grooved appearance. They run horizontally across the nails. These lines often show up when the area under your cuticle stops growing due to injury or severe illness. They appear because of different factors, such as circulatory diseases, diabetes, low blood pressure, malnutrition, grief, and shock. They may also appear on the nails of a person who has just undergone surgery. The surgery time can be determined from the precise location of the beau's lines on the fingernail.

Clubbing

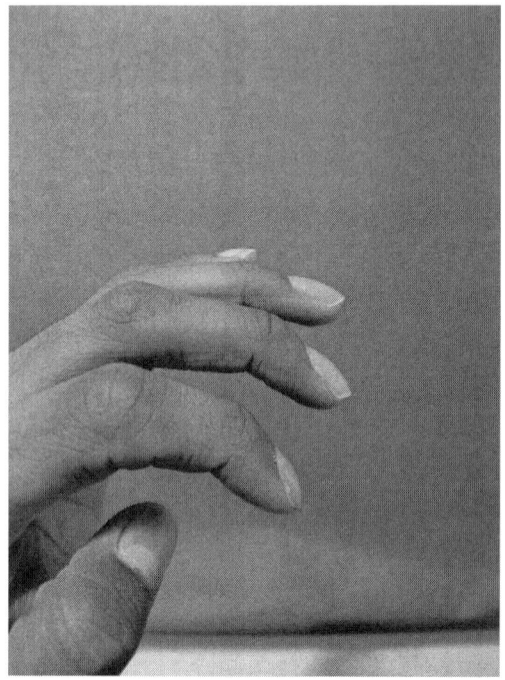

Fingernail clubbing occurs when the fingertip looks swollen, and the nail takes the shape of a dome, which means it's rounded and curved. The nail usually has a bluish tinge when fingernail clubbing happens. This condition may appear because of lung disease or low oxygen levels. If over three of a person's fingers have clubbed nails, it indicates that the disease or illness is advanced. Fingernail clubbing is linked to gastrointestinal diseases, cardiovascular diseases, and pulmonary diseases.

Spooned Nails

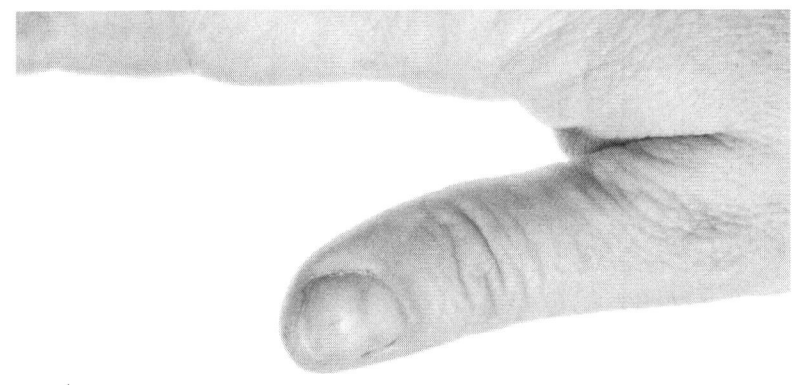

Spooned nails are concave nails, except they look like they have been chopped out. Spooned nails may indicate health problems from iron deficiency to thyroid, diabetes, and autoimmune disorders. An example is Raynaud's disease, which is a disorder that causes fingernail discoloration.

Sometimes, the nail plate becomes loose and separates from the skin. This usually happens as a response to trauma, infection, or injury. It could also signify a severe skin condition. Depending on your reading, loose fingernail also happens because of drug use and solvents.

Conclusively, change in fortune reflects on your nails almost immediately. Suppose you've recently experienced a change in your emotional and financial state and health. There, a good palmist can tell by examining your nails. If the changes are not yet effective but are on the way, this will reflect your nails. The nails work as a channel for all the energies you receive from the different planets. Therefore, always observe it carefully so you can monitor changes in your fortune and health condition.

The point is that just as the color and texture of your hand (palm) affects your reading, fingernail color and texture also has a significant impact on palm reading. An experienced and professional palmist can consider all factors before making conclusions. Next are the elements and how they define hand shape.

Chapter Seven: Reading the Elements - Hand Shape

Remember that we discussed the types of hand based on shape in a previous chapter. Well, there is another way of determining hand shape. Hand elements are an easy way of categorizing the different shapes of the hand. In the 1960s, Fred Gettings established this method of classifying hands based on elements. This method has since been used in palm reading. If you are new to palm reading, elements can make an excellent starting point for your readings. Starting with the hand's shape makes reading more straightforward and less complicated in a palm reading session. It is the quickest way to get a broad insight into your subject's nature and character, whether yourself or another person. By starting with the shape, the subject can be confident that you are talking about them.

One thing about humans is that we are all true to our hand type. There is often a behavioral pattern that people with earth hands follow. They are typically providing and steady. An air hand is found in people who enjoy mental stimulation. Fire hands mean that a person is active and volatile to an extent. A water hand suggests that the subject is sensitive, creative, and emotional. Understanding the four elements can influence your understanding of an individual and how they operate. More importantly, you must also understand their variations, complexities, and combination.

Air Hand

Air hands have squarish palms and long fingers. In appearance, they are often long and thin. Air is vital for life, even though we have a tendency to take it for granted. Many people don't even remember air unless it is windy or they have a respiratory condition. Air is critical to several aspects of life, including communication.

An air-handed individual is a thinker. Such a person functions in a world of thought. They are usually tall, which means they have light bones compared to other elements. Air hands are slightly looking, unlike earth hands, which are heavy and dense in appearance. The squarish palm in an air hand suggests a sense of reality, practicality, and structure. This means that air-handed people are systematic, strategic, and practical in their approach to problems. They are often consumed with logic, planning, ideas, structure, and thoughts.

Air-handedness indicates a quality of inquisitiveness. Air-handed people always want to know the how and why of a situation. Thus, they are ever trying to improve their knowledge and understanding of anything. They seek to refine and deepen. As a result, air-handed people love technical work over other kinds of work. Their curiosity and questioning nature may put them across as neurotic. Actually, they do have neurotic tendencies. Air-handed people love to engage in debates and logical arguments or discussions. They love to structure things and put them in perspective for others. This may also be why they like to exchange plans, ideas, and information with others. Being air-handed portrays a love for verbal and vocal exchanges, which is likely why air-handed individuals respond excellently to auditory information.

Air hands express a need for mentally stimulating conversations. So, an air-handed person will always look for intelligence and mental stimulation in their partner. They would rather be alone than being with someone they cannot engage in stimulating discussions with. They are non-conformist and quirky but in a cute way. Their eccentricity sometimes attracts people to them. Air hands make great instructors and teachers because of their profound communication skills. And they are more logical than emotional. They put thoughts above everything else, which often makes them neglect their emotions and sometimes their loved ones. Then they can't comprehend sensitivity in other people or know how to respond emotionally to situations.

These people often have an overworked nervous system, the result of multiple cognitive activities at once. They have a tendency to overthink things, so their nervous system is always at work. An air-handed person may be prone to mental disorders more than other elements due to their tendency to overthink and overanalyze situations. Without a clear procession of thoughts in their head, air-handed people become frustrated and noticeably stressed. Regardless of whatever information they receive, their first reaction is always "how" or "why?"

Air hands love to emphasize their level of thoughtfulness. They want you to know how much they think. They expect you to understand them as soon as they mention their level of logical thinking. Suppose you don't offer a constructive and positive topic they can really put their mind to. There, they may pick themselves apart mentally. Below are the physical features and qualities of air hands for easy identification.

- Square hands with long fingers
- Rounded fingertips
- Flat mounts and lightweight bones
- The middle finger is 7/8th long

- Prolonged, multiple lines on the palm
- Flexibility, adaptability, and passion
- Great communication skills
- Quick learners

Earth Hand

Like air hands, earth hands have a square palm. But unlike air hands, they have short fingers. So, when you see a combination of square palms and short fingers on a person, you can be confident they are earth hands. An earth hand is usually strong, plump, and firm, with fewer lines than other elements.

Earth-handed people are the most resilient types. They typically have strong drive and instincts. They combine practical with material and physical because they care about all three. As you can probably tell, they are down-to-earth, steady, and secure in themselves. They like to follow routine and crave stability, so they work in fields that offer stability. Earth hands love to provide just like the mother Earth is providing for all things on earth. An earth-handed person can be likened to the mother hand, the mountain, and the rock all at once. That is how much they enjoy being supportive of the people around them. They feel their best when they have a supporting role.

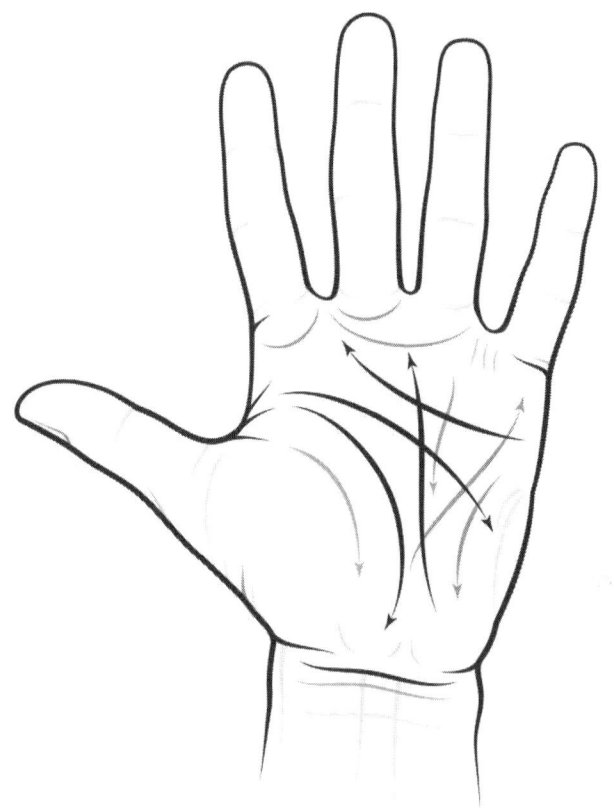

Earth hands also have immense physical strength and are tough and rugged. Manual activities provide the ultimate form of fulfillment for them. They love to take a hands-on approach to things, which is why they make good craftsmen. An earth-handed individual is strongly inclined to a stable lifestyle; they don't enjoy being rushed. They are reliable, honest, and grounded. They enjoy having a sense of rhythm to their daily activities. Structure cannot be given up for anything else. Their short fingers mean they are quick thinkers.

Earth hands call things as it is, which makes them blunter than most. They don't know how to color words to lessen the impact. Their broad, square palm indicates a dominating attitude. They want their presence to be felt in any environment they are in. Unlike the water and fire elements, they are rarely affected by their environment or surroundings. Moneymaking is usually the motivation and priority for work, yet they don't compromise practicality for this. They cannot work in a place where things aren't real, physical, and practical. Despite their liking for money, earth hands often do a good job. They are results-oriented.

An earth-handed person is loyal, stubborn, private, conservative, and productive. They hate to waste their resources, whether it is money, time, or energy. Some with earth-hands are highly unlikely to go for palm readings. Their liking for money is based on the need for something that provides stability and security. Earth hands are rarely academics because they would preferably use their hands instead of discussing intangible things. They don't like to talk about their feelings, so they build a fence between themselves and other people.

Earth hands have a robust and vital constitution. Their digestion is slow but firm, and they tend to store things. They eat less frequently than air hands. Earth is all about sturdiness and endurance, which means an air-handed person is likely to have strong stamina and look physically bulky. Suppose you need support from the elements. There, you are better off going to an earth type because they are reliable and trustworthy.

You can help an earth-handed individual by helping them establish a sense of routine and structure in their life. This will help them feel more grounded and secure. Also, they should engage in activities that require connecting with Mother Earth, such as building things, spending time outdoors, etc. More importantly, help them understand their tendency to resist change or get stuck in a routine. Here are physical features and qualities to identify an earth hand.

- Square palms and short fingers
- Big bones and stiff fingers
- Strong, firm mounts that are typically fleshy
- Few lines on the line
- Mounts are sometimes flat with stiff palms

- The middle finger is 3/4th of the palm
- Good with manual skills and activities
- Love to establish structure and routine
- Conservative, reserved, and mildly possessive
- Prone to volatile reactions if pushed

Water Hand

The water hand is recognizable by its narrow palm and long fingers. This combination positions someone in the world of thoughts, feelings, and emotions. The narrow palm means that the person is sensitive to their environment, while their long fingers mean they also spend time in their mind. Water element hands make a person caring, emotional, artistic, and intuitive. Water-handed people like to discuss their thoughts and feelings and those of other people. They can spend an entire day happily discussing and analyzing people's relationships.

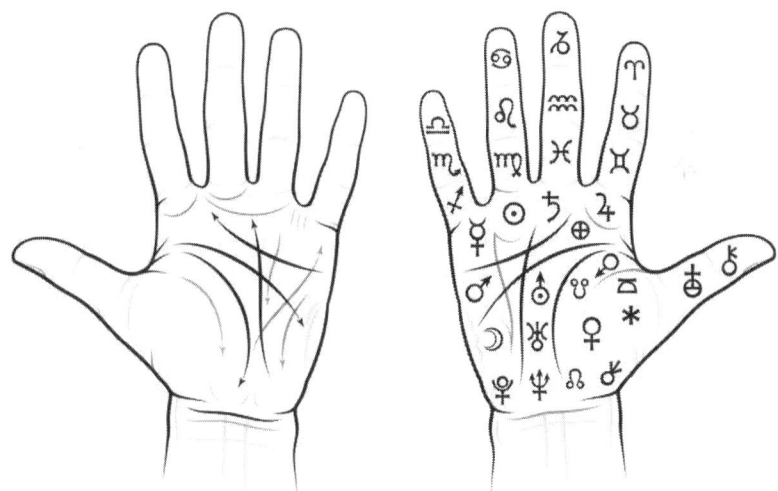

A water person takes people and relationships seriously. This contrasts with the fire element people who don't bother themselves with relationships or anything remotely similar. Water-handed people are at their best when helping people, especially with emotional problems. They love to be with people. Also, they make a lot of decisions based on their feelings. They value feelings much, which is why they care more about people than any other thing. They are empathetic. Thus, they make great therapists, healers, counselors, caretakers, helpers, etc. They are not materially inclined.

Water hands are also very in tune with their creative side. They need an outlet to express their creativity and artistic side regularly. Their creative side can take different forms, but the commonality is that they express their emotions through creative processes. They make good painters, writers, etc. – any activity that requires them to use their creativity is gratifying and satisfactory. Note that they need not be great at those creative activities they participate in. What matters is the feeling they benefit from the process.

Despite their creativity, water hands have difficulty succeeding in business compared to other elements. They don't do well with competition, which abounds in the business world. Succeeding in competitive fields is less likely for water-handed people. Fire hands do better in competitive environments.

To thrive and exceed, water hands need to be in an environment where they can do what they know how to do best, interact, socialize, and bond with people. They can't work well unless it is around people they can share their emotions with. People like this are open-minded and easily impressionable. They are prone to influence by their environment. Physically, they have a youthful look with a soft skin texture. They are likely to be chubby, and they put on weight quickly. They are easy-going and straightforward, and this reflects in their choices of outfits. Their hand lines are delicate and soft. They are also drawn to spiritual and ethereal practices.

A water-handed person is naturally inclined to live with their head in the clouds. So, they need someone to keep them grounded and structured. Advising them to establish a routine can be immensely helpful. Also, taking up hobbies involving physical activities, such as gardening, will help them live out of their heads more. It is a reliable platform for them to put their other qualities to work without stifling their creative side. The following are some physical features and traits that can help you identify a water-handed person.

- Narrow-shaped, rectangular palms and long fingers
- The middle finger is 7/8th of the palm, and fingers are longer than the palms' width
- Very flexible fingers and knuckles
- Fine, frail lines on the palms

Fire Hand

Narrow palms and short fingers define fire hands, and they are the opposite of water hand in this sense. The combination of palm and finger pegs down fire-handed people as people always seeking stimulation. The narrow palm portrays that their surroundings influence them. The short fingers mean they experience regular breaks in thinking. Their thoughts are generally short and brief.

Fire-handed people don't know how to stay without doing. They always have to be doing something. They feel their best when working on achieving something. Their burning passion makes it essential for them to fulfill their need for accomplishment. Fire hands love to get busy and physical. They can accomplish a lot in one day. If they can't let off steam through physical work, they may quickly become visibly frustrated. This could lead to aggressive behavior.

Naturally, fire hands are competitive, driven, and intense. This nature allows them to do well in sporty activities. They do well in any environment that encourages competition. You can always count on them to rise to the occasion and adapt to changes. A fire-handed person finds it difficult and frustrating to work with other people. Before they work with people, they have to be sure that they will take an active role. They don't like being passive. When you think fire hand, you think driven, competitive, passionate, excitable, and flashy. Typical fire hands love challenges.

The lines on their hands are distinctive in appearance. They usually have a hint of red, and they look deeply etched. When you see lines like this on anyone's hand, you can be sure that they have the fire element regardless of their fingers' length or palm shape. The lines suggest intensity and restlessness typically non-existent in other elements.

To help a fire-handed individual, it is best to find physical stimulation for them. For instance, if you are fire-handed, you should always have enough rest and relaxation to avoid burning yourself out. The best ways to unwind are swimming, yoga, walking, and other activities that involve "doing." The following are qualities and features to identify a fire hand.

- Narrow-shaped, rectangular palms with short fingers – similar to earth hand
- Red-colored palm indicating vibrancy and vitality
- Deeply etched, clear, and reddish handlines
- Takes work very importantly
- Goal and results-oriented

Based on the elements above are the different shapes of hands. Some people have hands with a mix of these qualities and features. They are called mixed hands, and they typically come with one dominating feature from one element. To read a mixed hand, make sure that you understand the four elements and what to look out for.

Chapter Eight: Reading the Fingers

Your finger lengths have different meanings and can tell you a lot about personality. Consider the length, the setting, the fingerprint pattern, and other essential features. But before you consider these things, you must know what each finger represents as well. Also, keep in mind that your fingers' proportion in relation to one another is crucial in readings. Each finger is representative of a character marking and the strength of that character. To break it down, this means that each of your fingers stands for quality and how strong that quality is.

PARTS OF THE HAND

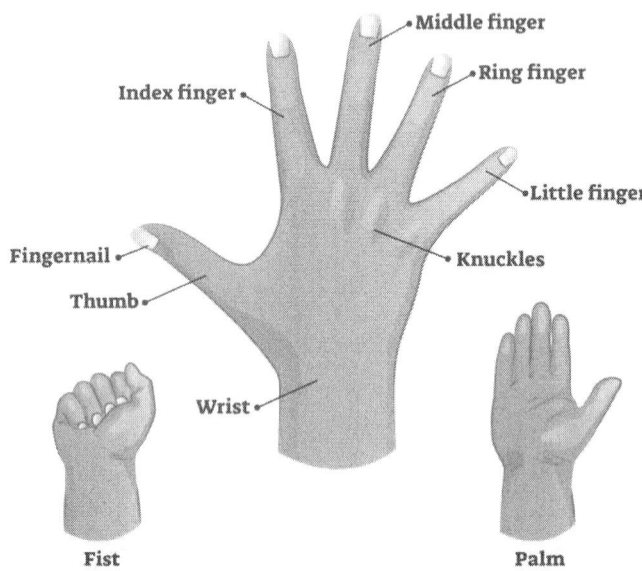

The forefinger marks ambition, drive, ego, and confidence.

The middle finger marks balance and discipline.

The ring finger marks creativity and emotional expressiveness.

The little finger marks communication skills.

- When the forefinger reaches up to the bottom of the middle fingernail, it indicates a balanced ego.
- If the ring finger reaches the base of the middle fingernail, that suggests balanced emotions.
- A forefinger that reaches past the base of the middle fingernail represents great confidence.
- When the ring finger reaches above the middle fingernail's root, that shows emotional and creative impulses.
- A forefinger that does not extend beyond the middle fingernail base portrays a lack of confidence.

- When the ring finger doesn't go beyond the middle fingernail base, it indicates blocked emotions.

- A middle finger that stands prominently apart from the other fingers suggests a severe and intense nature.

- A little finger that stands apart on your hand portrays an outspoken and independent personality.

Besides the fingers themselves, the signs you find on your fingers also significantly affect palm reading. They are significant in unraveling individuality and pattern of thinking. Below are the signs that often appear on the fingers.

- **Javelin:** This is an arrow-like sign that shows on the top phalange of the finger. When you see this on your finger or another person, it suggests high intellect and mental capacity. Such an individual succeeds under strenuous and adverse conditions. They can adapt to the needs of their environment, which makes it easy for them to be anywhere. They may develop heart problems in old age.

- **Tent:** If there is a tent-like sign on any of the phalanges, it indicates kind-heartedness and artistic ability. People like this can rise to the very top of society with their talents. But they also tend to take advantage of other people to facilitate their rise to the top. The tent sign on the finger shows mental imbalance and troubled family background.

- **Circle:** If you have a circle sign on your hand, it is considered auspicious. It means you are independent-minded. You strive to be original in everything you do. It also shows an inclination towards liberalism and modern beliefs.

- **Triangle:** A triangle sign on the finger portrays mystery. People with this sign tend to be mysterious in the way they think and act. They love to be alone, and you may describe them as orthodox. They enjoy working on their bodies to make them stronger, so they may take bodybuilding activities as a hobby.

• **Arch**: An arch on the finger signifies laziness and suspiciousness. Such a person may be distrustful of others. They don't believe in themselves or the people around them. As a result, they like to create a form of illusion around themselves. They often thrive in careers that revolve around mysticism, such as a detective.

• **Star:** This sometimes appears as the cross sign. It is an indication of fortune and good luck. If a star-like sign appears on your finger, don't be surprised when people send you money and gifts unexpectedly. Financially, you are always happy and fulfilled.

• **Rectangle:** A person with a rectangle sign on their phalange is laborious, prosperous, and genuinely happy in life.

• **Net:** A net-like sign on the finger portrays challenges, obstacles, and difficulties on the path to fulfilling life's purpose. Some with this sign will overcome every blockade on their way to success and come out unscathed. But they are usually less comfortable and happy with their life. This sign often appears on the hands of culprits or petty criminals.

Some people have a combination of these signs on their fingers. When this happens, such people enjoy the combined meanings of the signs. To make an accurate analysis of whatever sign (s) you see on your fingers, carefully consider all the meanings compared to one another.

The way a person wears rings on their fingers can show you their inner character, rather than the one they express to people around them. If someone wears several rings on their hand, it could mean that they have an emotional fence between them and other people. It could also mean that they depend on external validation to keep pushing.

- A ring on the forefinger indicates ambition and a need to boost the ego.

- A ring on the middle finger suggests a materialistic and worldly nature.

- Wearing a ring on the ring finger is conventional. But suppose the ring is more than one or more prominent than usual. In that case, it points to the presence of creative and emotional frustration.

- On the little finger, a ring portrays difficulties in expressing sexuality.

There are gaps between your fingers. These gaps or spaces are called interdigital folds. They reflect thinking, fortune, behavior, and achievement. To check the gap between your fingers and their meanings, you have to relax your hand and keep it flat on a surface. Make sure there is no pressure.

- A broad and equal gap between the fingers represents love, boldness, enthusiasm, freedom, and action.

- A narrow space between the ring and middle fingers reveals a penchant for freedom. It also suggests an inability to approach matters cautiously. With this kind of gap, you are the person that enjoys making a long-term and detailed plan for your future. You are also quite thoughtful.

- If you have a vast space between your ring and middle finger, it suggests that you don't like being restrained. You don't worry about the future because you are in good material condition. You procrastinate and leave things till the last minute.

- A wide space between the middle finger and index finger suggests independent thinking. It means you don't like it when people interrupt or interfere with your thoughts. You are stubborn and strong-willed.

- If you have a vast space between the little finger and ring finger, it suggests that you don't like being under control. You want to be your own person without interference from anybody.

- You may be suffering from fatigue if your fingertips tremble whenever you open your hands. It may also be a sign of sexual dysfunction.

Another way is to put your hand in a relaxed state and then fold the fingers close together to read the gaps.

- Little to no space between the fingers suggests that you are conservative, practical, thrifty, thoughtful, and careful. Yet, you are also stubborn, selfish, and inflexible. Soft fingers with no space mean you love steady work and enjoying money.

- Wide gaps between your fingers indicate ambitiousness and recklessness. You tend to be rigid in your ways, which may lead to economic and financial losses. You are somewhat thoughtless. Wide-spaced fingers with a heart line that runs across your middle finger suggest extravagance and lavishness.

- A vast space between your middle finger and index finger shows you don't adhere to rules because you enjoy freethinking. It also indicates a healthy level of self-awareness. You respect other people's feelings and actions, even though you don't necessarily care about them. You live an independent life.

- Your ring finger tells you about your relationship luck. The middle finger reveals career development. If you have a narrow space between both fingers, it means that your romantic relationship and career are closely knitted. For example, your career may cause you to end a relationship. Or you reach a significant career accomplishment due to your relationship. A wide space between both fingers suggests a reckless nature and a lack of a future plan. If space is even wider, it means that your relationships will suffer twists and turns. You may regularly participate in conflicts with your partner.

- A wide space between the little finger and ring finger indicates poor luck. You find it hard to meet benefactors or get help from people. No matter your condition, you are the only person you can count on. And you need to improve your interpersonal relationships and learn to respect others more. A more expansive space with a slightly bent little finger indicates a poor relationship with your kids in old age.

- If the space between the index finger and thumb is wide, it means you are broad-minded and gentle by nature. But a narrow space suggests narrow-mindedness, dependency, and a need for control. If you relax and open your hand and you get a vast space between the thumb and index finger, it suggests that you love your freedom.

The length of a finger can provide varying information about a person's character. You can use the length to get more in-depth information about yourself or a subject in palm reading. Below explains what each finger tells you based on the length.

- **Index Finger**: In palm reading, the index finger represents a desire for power and domination. The longer the index, the stronger the desire. Individuals with long index fingers are typically ambitious, aggressive, and indomitable. They climb up to positions of authority quickly. If the index finger is about the middle finger's length, it suggests a harsh and ostentatious personality. Someone with this length spends as much as they earn. Saving is hard for them, so they may need to learn to control their spending and consumption habits. Longer index fingers also portray an enterprising nature. People with this finger have excellent management and communication skills. So, they can establish good social and interpersonal relationships with others - although they may also be controlling. A shorter index finger suggests jealousy and competitiveness. People with short index fingers have good luck with love, but they may experience hardships in other aspects of their lives.

- **Middle Finger:** As you already know, the middle finger is the longest of the four fingers. It represents fate and destiny, and the longer, rounder, and straighter your middle finger, the better for you. A straight, round, and long middle finger indicates a good destiny and fortune. If you have this kind of finger, you will experience favors in your career, relationships, and finances. A short and oblique middle finger with leanings towards the index finger indicates persistence in work. If it leans more to the ring finger, it suggests an obsession with family. An unevenly thick middle finger points to impulsivity and impatience. Some with this type of finger need to learn to control their emotions to avoid doing things they might regret. If the middle finger's length is inches above the other fingers, it is a sign of prosperity, wealth, and health in middle age. A relatively short middle finger almost the same length as other fingers suggests impatience with work. Such a person changes work frequently. But they also have a stable financial condition and love life.

- **Ring Finger:** This finger represents romantic and familial relationships. A ring finger with leanings to the little finger represents someone supportive of their children. When it leans to the middle finger, it portrays a responsible and supportive family member. A ring finger that is almost the same length as the middle finger shows love for betting and gambling. A relatively long ring finger means you have unique insights into your career. But a short ring finger suggests individuality and down-to-earth nature. People like this are steady, and they rarely take risks.

- **Little Finger**: The little finger has to with your kids and generation. If you have a short and crooked little finger, it is a sign that your children may cause you to worry in the future. And the little finger also represents eloquence and wisdom. Physiognomists call it the *second thumb.*

Note that throughout this chapter, I have mentioned bent or crooked fingers several times. Quickly, let's look into what crooked or bent fingers mean for the owner.

What does it mean when a person has bent fingers?

It is not uncommon for people to have slightly crooked or bent fingers. The crookedness of a finger portrays variance in the traits that the finger represents. Sometimes, a slightly bent finger may lean away or towards another finger, which is straight. When this happens, that finger portrays the present rather than something from the past or the future. A bent finger gives some of its strength to the finger beside it. When the whole finger has a curve, it means that the finger gains strength from the other finger.

In other words, the finger bent towards another finger is strengthening the other finger's qualities. So, if your ring finger is bent towards the little finger, it is giving it strength. But if it leans towards the middle finger, it is drawing strength from the middle finger.

A crooked index finger curves towards the middle finger and, when this happens, it can mean a couple of different things. First, it may depict a pattern of uncertainty over your direction and the decisions you make in life. It may also suggest a need for security and stability in your life. Another possible meaning is that a person has a jealous personality and is insecure in their relationships. When all of your four fingers are inwardly bent, this shows a timid or insecure personality. Also, it could mean that a person is shrewd and selfish. When fingers are bent inward together, it shows a lack of openness to others. People with inwardly bent fingers may have a distorted view of reality. This could push them to unlawful or corruptive activities, particularly when they also have a short middle finger.

A crooked ring finger is a sign of shrewdness. If it curves towards the middle finger, it absorbs certain qualities and strength from the other finger. It is typically present in artists. Also, it shows a serious and responsible nature with a high presence of creativity. An artist with a crooked ring finger may cheat their ways to opportunities. If the middle finger slightly leans towards the ring finger, it suggests limited creative expression. This could be due to familial responsibilities and commitments. If the ring finger leans away from the middle finger, this is the opposite of creativity. It suggests someone quiet and rarely expressive. Such a person enjoys living alone and staying away from others. They are compulsive about things that matter to them. Otherwise, they don't care generally.

Usually, the middle finger is long and straight. But it can be bent in some people. When you have a bent middle finger, it suggests a leaning towards the extraordinary. Someone with a bent middle finger rarely follows routines. They are also not very good at decision-making. This all depends on the direction the finger is curved towards. It is difficult to spot the bent in the middle finger because it is subtle. But you can see it by looking from the back of your palm. The meanings change based on the direction. When it bends towards the ring finger, it gives strength to a person's creative nature. It also indicates a pattern of uncertainty, pressure, and depression. If it leans towards the index finger, which is rare, it suggests an extroverted personality.

The little finger can be curved from birth or as one grows up. The curve of the little finger can indicate confidence in communication. A little finger curved from birth tells you about character, while one that curves in the growing years tells about a person's history. Generally, a bent little finger shows how a person communicates with others. When the pinkie leans towards the ring finger, it absorbs from it. This suggests a level of alertness, tact, and shrewdness. When it leans away from the ring finger, it shows a highly diplomatic and independent-minded person.

Also, the way your fingers are set into your palm reflects specific personality traits. When you have evenly set fingers, it means you are confident and successful. An uneven set of fingers shows a lack of confidence, particularly with low-set fingers. An arched setting of the fingers means you have a well-balanced personality.

Reading the Thumb

The thumb represents your whole hand. Much importance is attached to it in palm reading. The thumb is considered more important than the hand lines in palmistry. Your thumb can reveal your whole identity without consulting other features. Hence, it is considered the root of the hand. It is also called the center of willpower. The top phalange of the thumb stands for logic, while the lower phalange stands for willpower.

The longer the first phalange of the thumb directly determines a person's strong-will. A person with a prolonged thumb phalange is self-willed. With a longer phalange, such a person has no desire to work. A shorter phalange means weaker self-will. If the thumb's front appears squarish, it shows someone competent in legal matters and highly respected. A wide front of the thumb means such a person is obstinate. If the forepart is long, the person has antisocial tendencies. If the second phalange of the thumb is long, it means that a person is smart, careful, and social. Such a person is highly respected and considered of importance. A short phalange suggests someone that acts without forethought. This person may act clumsily due to a lack of reasoning.

There are seven types of thumbs. They include:

- **Long Thumb:** Self-willed, self-dependent, and controlling. Considers intelligence to be vital. Typically interested in engineering and mathematics.

- **Short Thumb:** Easily influenced by others. More emotional than intelligent. Typically interested in music, poetry, and painting.

- **Stiff Thumb:** Alert, self-aware, and obstinate. Ability to keep secrets. Lacks emotions but is highly intelligent.

- **Flexible Thumb:** Interested in gathering wealth. Capable of adapting to circumstances.

- **Obtuse-Angled Thumb:** Gentle and sweet-tempered. Typically interested in music and artistic activities.

- **Acute-Angled Thumb:** Indolent, lavish, and extravagant. Attracted to corrupt activities.

- **Right-Angled Thumb:** Short-tempered but reliable. Hardworking yet stays neutral in relationships. Vengeful nature.

Those are the different types of thumbs and what they mean. When reading the thumb, consider the length and shape.

Chapter Nine: Reading the Mounts and the Plains

Mounts are some of the most challenging things to read in palmistry. They are the bumps of flesh on your palms. Reading them is an advanced form of palm reading that takes quite a time to learn. They are close to your wrist. They are called mounts because they look like mountains on the palm. In palmistry, we have multiple mounts, all of which are named after the planets. Each mount represents a different character in a person.

The defining features of the planets are found in their corresponding Mounts. The most prominent planet in the horoscope tends to be the most prominent on the palm. By reading how far-developed a person's mounts are, you can learn about their lifestyle, romantic inclination, career, and other things. The seven mounts in palmistry are:

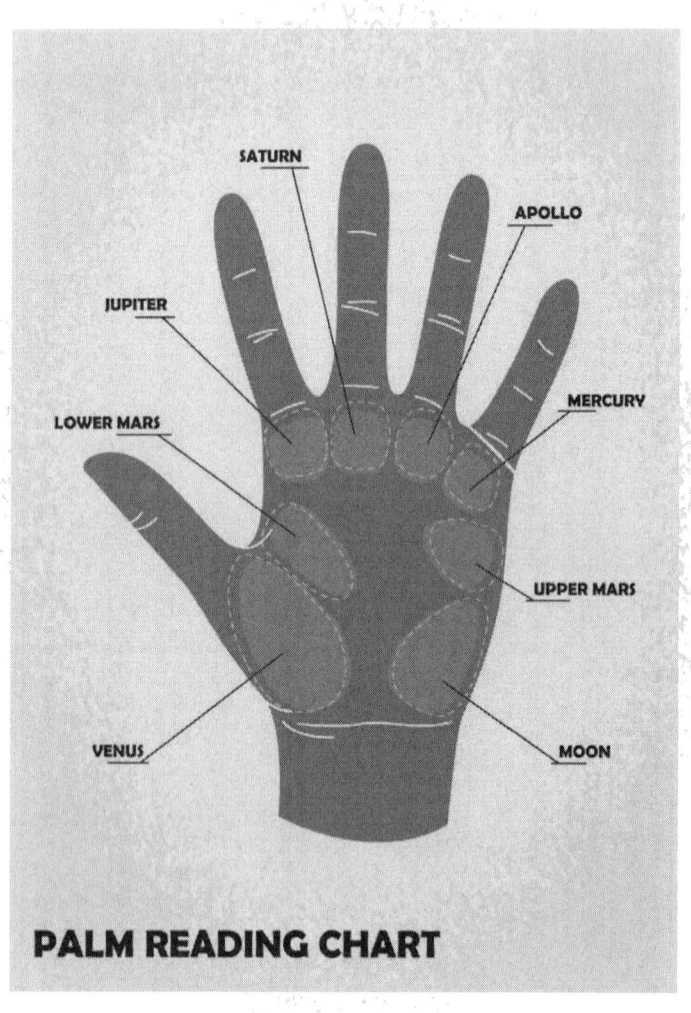

PALM READING CHART

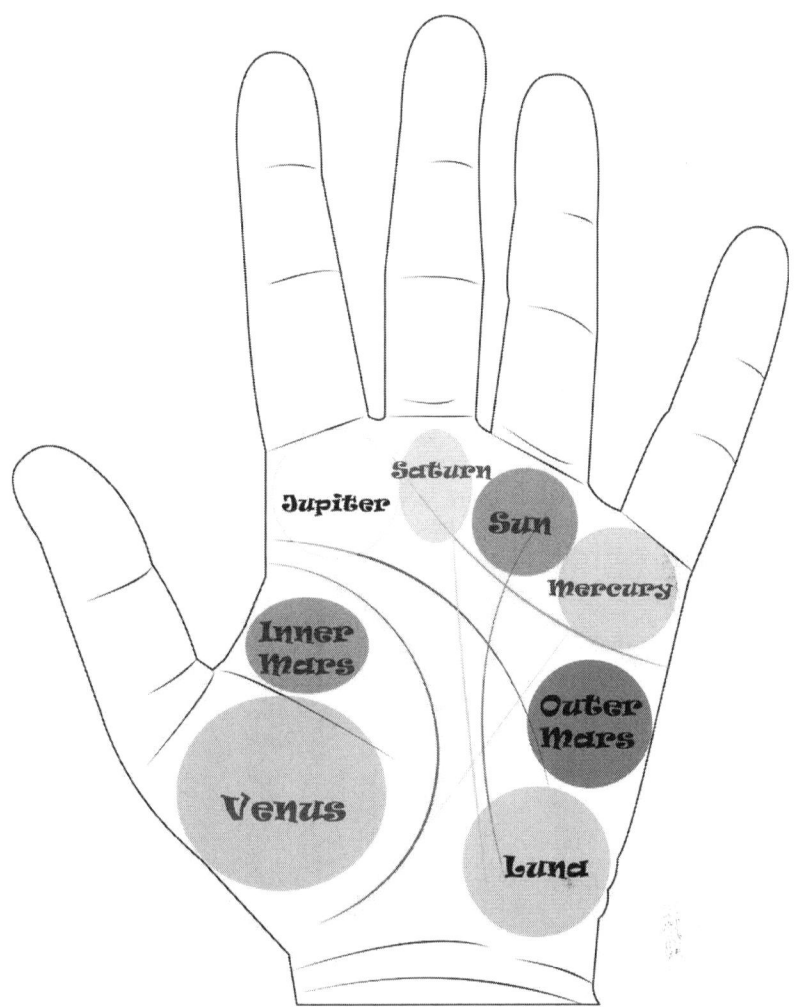

Mount of Jupiter

Location: Base of the index finger, just above the Mount of Mars.

Quality: Represents leadership, authority, power, and organization.

The Mount of Jupiter is crucial to progress. It is said to help facilitate progress in life. A well-developed and prominent Mount of Jupiter is found in people who possess godly qualities. Such people care deeply about self-respect. They are always ready to help others. They are usually learned and intelligent. Rarely do they get bothered or pressured by difficult conditions. Those who work as Justices in the high courts tend to have a fully developed Mount of Jupiter. They can influence the public in their favor. They also tend to be religious-minded.

If Jupiter is not well developed or prominent, the qualities described above are sorely lacking. Physically, someone with an under-developed Mount of Jupiter has a healthy and ordinary-looking body. They are kind-natured and always have a smile on their face. They are likely to be more respected than wealthy. A person can also have an over-developed Jupiter. When this happens, such a person is overly proud, selfish, and self-conceited. The absence of the Mount of Jupiter on an individual's palms suggests that they have a hard time commanding others' respect. They also lack self-respect for themselves. Even from loved ones, this person does not get attention and love.

Mount of Saturn

Location: Based at the root of the middle finger.

Qualities: Represents intelligence, integrity, responsibility, and duty.

Developing the Mount of Saturn points to extraordinary tendencies in a person. When this mount is well developed, it means that the person is realistic, independent, friendly, and mathematically skilled. It also indicates good fortune. But an individual with a developed Mount of Saturn may be aloof towards others. They are set on achieving their goals, and this pushes them away from family. Such a person is usually engrossed in work. They also have a suspecting nature. They make great scientists, engineers, chemists, etc. An under-developed Mount of Saturn means that a person is superficial, disorganized, judgmental, lonely, and depressed.

Someone like this has suicidal tendencies. If over-developed, a person is isolated, cynical, pessimistic, distrusting, overcautious, and stubborn. This keeps them away from forming healthy and mutually beneficial relationships. An individual without a Mount of Saturn has no importance in life. But they might get special recognition or achieve something special in life.

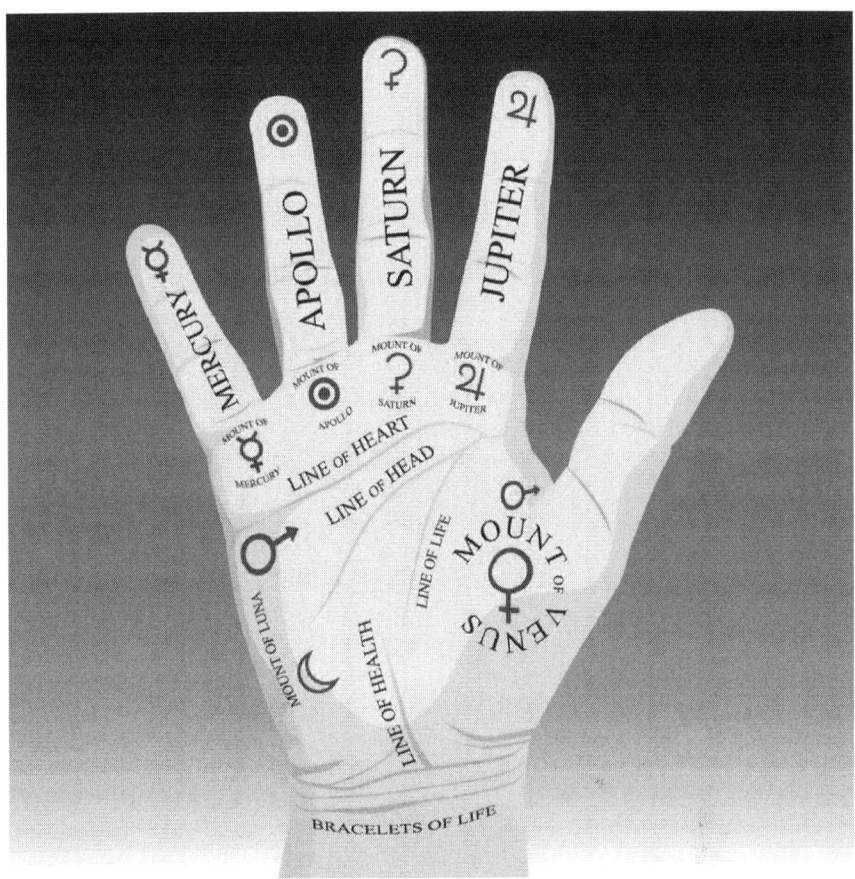

Mount of Sun

Location: Based at the root of the ring finger.

Qualities: Represents leadership, wealth, self-assurance, confidence, masculinity, and passion.

The Mount of Sun is also called Apollo. It indicates the level of success of an individual. A prominent Mount of Sun indicates that a person is famous and genius. It shows a high probability of achieving high status in life. A well-developed Mount of Sun often has a pink look. Someone with a prominent mount is typically cheerful and sociable. They love to work in proximity to others. Such a person may become a successful painter, artist, or musician. They are natural geniuses. Also, they are straightforward in their dealings with others.

A well-developed Mount of Sun portrays self-confidence, kindness, gentleness, and grandeur. An underdeveloped mount means an individual is dull, inconsistent, introverted, and a bad decision-maker. This person will find it hard to succeed in any field. An over-developed Mount of Sun shows a hot-tempered and antagonistic individual. This person may be envious, proud, quarrelsome, and lavish. The absence of the mount points to an ordinary person destined for an ordinary life.

Mount of Mercury

Location: Base of the little finger.

Qualities: Represents logic, practicality, adaptability, and wisdom.

The Mount of Mercury is often associated with affluence and materialistic prosperity. A well-developed mount means an individual is quick-witted, flexible, mentally strong, organized, sensible, and excellent at reading others. It also means that a person has excellent communication skills. Such people are experts in Psychology. Their understanding of human psychology makes them successful in business. If the mount is under-developed, it portrays negativity, shyness, an inability to communicate effectively, and low financial success. An over-developed mount is found in greedy, materialistic people and will do anything for money. If the Mount of Mercury is absent, it indicates a person might be impoverished for the rest of their life. They cannot amass wealth and make money.

Mount of Venus

Location: Base of the thumb, just next to the Mount of Inner Mars.

Qualities: Represents beauty, luxury, love, sensuality, and appearance.

The Mount of Venus represents things that concern passion. People with well-developed Venus can adequately enjoy the world and its luxuries. They are beautiful, classy, and civilized. They are healthy and influential, and they are also bold and courageous. Someone with the Mount of Venus is said to enjoy the finer things in life. They have good fortune with wealth, love, and relationships. But when the mount is under-developed, it suggests that a person is lackluster, cold-hearted, overly critical, and has no interest in romance. The person may also be weak-natured and cowardly.

An over-developed Mount of Venus suggests that a person is promiscuous, superficial, materialistic, overindulgent, and covetous. Such a person always seeks instant gratification due to their lack of willpower. The absence of the mount means the person is inclined towards an ascetic lifestyle. They have no interest in family life.

Mount of Mars

Location: Center of the palm.

Qualities: Represents masculine energy, action, aggressiveness, and conflict.

The palm has three different Mars, all of which are located in the center of the palm. You have the Negative Mars, Positive Mars, and Plain of Mars. Each of these Mars deals with specific aspects of the qualities listed above.

The Negative Mars, also called the Mount of Inner Mars, is between Jupiter and Venus. This Mount represents one positive and one negative trait—enthusiasm and aggression. A well-developed Mount of Inner Mars means that a person is enthusiastic, adventurous, courageous, and healthy. An under-developed mount suggests indecisiveness, uncertainty, timidity, limited emotional expression, and a lack of self-esteem. An over-developed mount suggests that a person is quick-tempered, aggressive, egotistical, and argumentative.

Positive Mars is called the Mount of Outer Mars. It is based between Venus and Luna and signifies a person's temperament and resistance level. A well-developed Mount of Outer Mars indicates strong character, courage, good health, and balance; under-developed, it represents trouble with emotional expression. An over-developed mount means that a person is defiant and stubborn.

The Plain of Mars is also called the Middle of Mars. It is between the Inner and Outer Mars. The mount here is typically not big, so the interpretations often differ. A thick Plain of Mars indicates sociability, energy, and possible rebellion. Under-developed suggests a quick-tempered and self-centered nature. A dip in the Middle of Mars indicates a calm temperament and a patient nature.

Mount of Moon

Location: Base of the palm beside the little finger.

Qualities: Represents emotion, intuition, creativity, and imagination.

The Mount of Moon makes a person highly imaginative and emotional. A fully developed mount signifies a love of nature and beauty. Someone with this tends to live in a dream world because of his or her ability to imagine. Such a person is a dreamer, a lover of nature, psychic, compassionate, and intuitive. They also love water. Under-developed Moon means a person is introverted and loves to be alone. It also signifies a lack of innovation, conservatism, and pessimism.

If the Mount is over-developed, the person is over-imaginative, sentimental, overly emotional, and possibly delusional. This person lives in a fantasy world that they've created in their head.

Checking Your Health Through the Mounts

The mounts of your palm contain information about your life and health. By reading the mounts, you can keep yourself updated on the state of your health. For centuries, palmistry has been used to diagnose diseases in people. So, how do you check your health through the palm mounts?

- The Mount of Luna, also the Mount of Moon, is the direct mount containing information about mental illness, obesity, and women's diseases generally.
- The Mount of Venus is responsible for allergy, kidney disease, stomach disease, and dampness.
- The Mount of Mars contains information about inflammation, blood pressure, fever, and arteriosclerosis.
- The Mount of Jupiter is in charge of stroke, rheumatism, dizziness, and hepatobiliary disease.
- The Mount of Saturn controls depression, rheumatism, biliary disease, hemorrhoids, and osteoporosis.
- The Mount of Apollo regulates diseases relating to the heart and blood circulation.
- The Mount of Mercury is responsible for hearing disorders, bipolar disorder, language, and the nervous system

To use the palm to diagnose diseases and illnesses, you have to examine the mounts' thickness with the hand lines. Usually, when you are in good health, the mount looks thick, rosy, and prominent. If it looks different from this, it could be a sign of an impending or present illness.

The Mount of Venus indicates the health of your stomach and digestive system, and your spleen. If you see bulging blue veins on this mount, it could be a sign of stomach illness or poor digestion. Messy lines on the Mount suggest a vulnerability to reproductive system illnesses. With feathery lines, it suggests a disease relating to the nervous system.

The Mount of Jupiter is in charge of functions relating to the stomach, gall, and liver. If the Mount is bloated with a couple of messy lines, it shows a vulnerability to hepatobiliary and stomach diseases. Also, this Mount corresponds to the heart and the liver. If it appears bloated with negative signs, it suggests susceptibility to cardiovascular disease.

The Mount of Mercury is in charge of respiratory and reproductive functions. Messy lines on the mount could mean a proneness to respiratory diseases and digestive system diseases.

The Mount of Mars takes charge of reproductive and renal functions. Messy lines on this mount mean one is vulnerable to diseases linked to the urinary, reproductive, and respiratory systems.

The Mount of Saturn takes charge of heart functions and blood circulation. A star sign on Saturn implies a proneness to hypertension or high blood pressure. If it is bloated with scattered lines, it indicates susceptibility to hemorrhoids, paralysis, nervous system disease, etc.

The Mount of Apollo is in charge of sensory functions. If you find tiny lines on this mount, it could sign eye disease or neurasthenia. Messy lines on Apollo could mean vulnerability to heart disease, aneurysm, visual neurasthenia, etc.

Finally, the Mount of Luna corresponds with respiratory and gynecological functions. Messy lines on Luna means that a person may be susceptible to respiratory diseases. Also, if a deep vertical line accompanies the Mount of Luna, it suggests possible numbness in the limbs.

Note: Do not use the palms to make medical conclusions; consult with a licensed medical professional after a reading. Doing this will help you gain more insight into your health. Also, you can corroborate if everything you interpreted is accurate or not.

Chapter Ten: Reading the Lines

Look at your palm. How many lines do you see? Like me, you probably see three significant lines and several other minor ones. Actually, that is what anyone would see when they look at their palm. Whether big or small, thick or thin, every line on your palm is vital in determining the speed of your life force. Therefore, to make a good palmist, you must know how to study each line on your palm critically.

Every person has three primary lines on the palm, plus others considered minor or secondary lines. The three major lines are the Life Line, the Head Line, and the Heart Line. The Fate Line and Marriage Line are sometimes categorized as significant lines, but the above three come before them. These three lines are significant because they hold valuable information about each aspect of your life that shapes who you are as a person. To aid your understanding, we will discuss each major line separately.

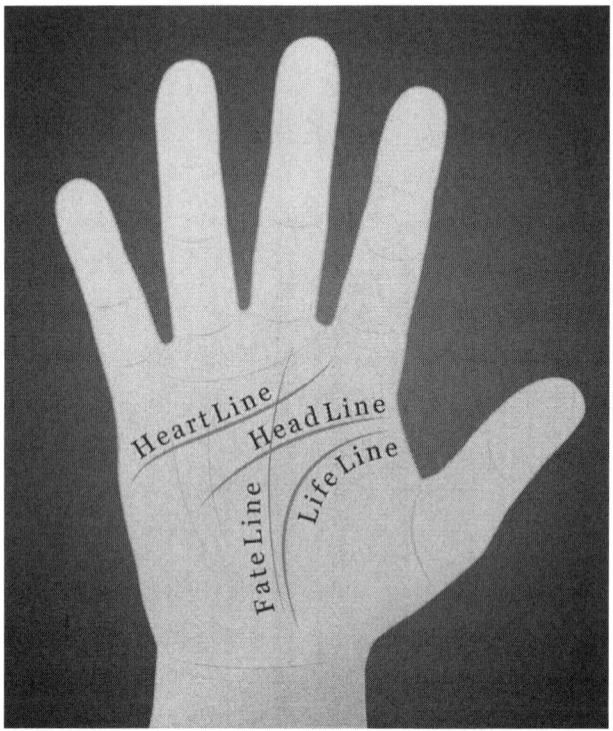

Lifeline

Description: The lifeline begins from the palm's edge between the index finger and the thumb. From there, it extends towards the wrist and stops at the base of the thumb.

The lifeline is perhaps the most intriguing line to study on the palm. Many people go to palmists just to read their palm lines. The lifelines are often called the age line or the paternal lifeline. It represents multiple facets of human life, but the general misconception is that the lifeline determines a person's mortality. Many people believe that the lifeline can tell them how long they will live. This is a case of partial misunderstanding. The lifeline reflects a person's life force, energy, and physical vitality. Also, one can use it to check for accidents or severe illnesses during one's lifetime.

If you can clearly see other lines on your palm, but the lifeline is almost absent, this is a negative sign. It suggests that a short life and poor health. If you have no lifeline, it means you will be prone to accidents and sicknesses throughout your lifetime.

- A long, deeply etched, and tender lifeline means you are highly resistant to diseases. It also means you are full of vital energy.

- A short lifeline shows you are vulnerable to illness. It does not mean that one has a short lifespan, contrary to what many believe. Personality-wise, a short lifeline shows you are down-to-earth and full of integrity.

- A thick lifeline suggests that you are subjected to a life of physical labor.

- A vague lifeline indicates that you get sick quickly. It also means that your career may not pick up until your middle years.

- A straight lifeline that sticks closely to the thumb signifies limited energy and vitality. You may get tired and dehydrated quickly.

- A semicircular lifeline close to the base of your thumb means you are full of energy and vigor. You are also enthusiastic.

- A doubled lifeline that runs parallel to another line is also a sign of healthy vitality. It shows you are resistant to disease and illness. And you get adequate mental and emotional support from family members.

Most times, lifelines come with markings and signs. These marks are instrumental in interpreting the meaning of the lifeline. So, pay close attention to them when doing a palm reading.

- **Chained**: If your lifeline has a marking similar to a chain, this could indicate poor health. It means you may have a weak digestive system and repeatedly suffer from shattered health.

- **Island**: An island on the lifeline indicates accidents, illnesses, or hospitalization at specific times during your lifetime. The severity of the accident or illness depends on the size of the island marking.

- **Broken:** The lifeline is sometimes broken. When this is the case, it means you might endure a major illness, accident, or disaster in your life. The wider the interval between the broken lines, the longer the duration of the illness. If the broken lines overlap, it suggests you will recover from the illness. If you observe a short line below or above the broken lifeline, it means you will fully recover from the severe illness.

- **Branches**: A branched marking above the lifeline represents diligence, positivity, and optimism. If the branched markings are plenty, it shows you have ambitious and lofty plans. But too many lines means you get nowhere due to too many ideas. Branched markings that go downward on the lifeline imply that your physical health is declining. You may feel lonely and tired all the time.

- **Forks**: If your lifeline looks forked at the end, it suggests you will be busy in your middle and late years. This may be because of developing your career.

- **Tridents**: If tridents appear at the end of your lifeline, it signifies you as a traveler. You will enjoy traveling to different parts of the world.

- **Tassels:** These often appear at the beginning of the lifeline. They indicate loneliness in old age due to the absence of children.

Other markings you may find around your lifeline include crosses, stars, etc.

Heart Line

Description: The heart line starts from under the little finger, runs across the palm, and ends just below the point where the middle finger and the index finger join.

The heart line is also called the love line. It symbolizes your attitude to love and the quality of love you give out and receive. Whether your feelings are complicated or straightforward, your affections are deep or not, your love life is smooth or rocky, and the quality of your interpersonal relationships can all be deducted from your love line. Generally, a good heart line is deep, curved, clear, and unbroken. It also extends to the midpoint of your middle and index fingers. When you have a line like this, it means you will enjoy a quality and good love life. If the line has three forks at the end, that is even better. It means you will have good-hearted friendships.

A short love line only extends to the middle finger, so your love life may not be all that. If your love life stops under the middle finger, it shows you are a self-centered and narrow-minded person. You are likely to act without weighing the consequences. These traits make you become ostracized by people, which leads to loneliness. Your relationships are generally not smooth.

A long heart line extends to the edge of your palm from under your pinkie and the midpoint of your middle finger and index finger. This length of heart line means you are a straightforward person. Career-wise, you go through a lot of hardship but come out on top. You may experience significant upheavals in your relationships. You often come out of a relationship hurting. If the love line stops at the Mount of Jupiter, it symbolized an abundance of love and success. If it ends between Jupiter and Saturn, it means you will experience true love in the pure sense.

- **Curved:** A love line that curved upward suggests you are a romantic. You know how to create the perfect romantic experience for your partner. You also have dexterity with your use of words. A downward curve suggests a weak character. You make other people feel uneasy around you. It also means you will experience twists and turns in your marriage.

- **Straight:** A straight love line means you are conservative, stable, affable, mild-tempered, and approachable. You tend to play a passive role in your relationships due to shyness. If the heart line is moderately long and clear with no break, you will have a stable and happy family with the one you love.

Markings on the heart line can change the meanings and your interpretation.

- **Branches:** If you have branches that split at the end of your heart line, it means you are willing to sacrifice for love. Multiple branches at the end mean you are always in love and may clinch true love. Trident at the end suggests universal fraternity, but you often pretend to be challenging in your love life. Two to three upward branches indicate an abundance of love and charm.

- **Forks:** Double forks at the beginning of the heart line signify that you may experience marital disputes.

- **Island:** An island marking on your heart line suggests emotional distress or changes.

- **Broken:** If the heart line is broken, it means you will experience considerable setbacks in your love life. If the broken line has an extended interval, it suggests instability in relationships or marriage. If the break is under the pinkie, it indicates stress over money and material things. You may find it difficult to experience true love because of materialistic beliefs. If the break is under the space between your little and ring fingers and the line ends below your middle finger and index finger's joining point, that means you might experience a failed marriage. After that phase, though, you can have your own true love and settle in a happy marriage. A break just below the middle finger also points to an unhappy marital life. You may divorce your partner over a trivial issue.

• **Broken Palm:** If you find you have no heart line, this could be due to an overlap of the headline and the heart line. This is called the Simian Crease or the Single Transverse Palmar Crease. This line represents a stubborn nature.

• **Chained:** If the heart line has the marking of an iron chain, it indicates sentiments. A lot of chain markings suggest emotional entanglements. You may endure marital crises in your middle age.

• **Triangles:** If you observe triangular markings on your heart line, which indicates disease or interference from another in your marriage or relationship. Suppose the triangle is just above the heart line. There, it indicates that you are fickle and likely to be the third person in other people's marriage. Below the line means you might experience an accident on a date with your loved one.

• **Square:** If a square appears on your love line, it means you will become emotionally depressed. This could even lead to suicidal thoughts.

• **Doubled:** A doubled heart line means you are emotionally expressive. You don't mind being an initiative when it comes to love. But it also means you have the tendency to be in two relationships together.

• **Crossed:** A cross on the heart line means that your career may be held back by your love life.

If you find many short lines cutting through your heart line, that is a sign of unhappiness and pain due to relationship and love failures. After middle age, you may not be able to experience love.

Headline

Description: The headline begins from the edge of the palm between the thumb and index finger and stretches across the palm. It stops in the middle of the lifeline and the love line.

Also called the wisdom line, the headline reveals the extent of your wisdom, belief, thinking, ability, creativity, attitude, and strain capacity. It also shows your abilities in terms of memory, self-control, etc. Generally, the headline should have a deep and thin appearance. That is good for anybody. The headline's meaning can be affected by the length, curve, chains, crosses, and stars that appear on, below, or above it.

A long headline extends and stops under the pinkie. If you have this line, it indicates that you have a clear and sharp mind. You are good at thinking and responding. Due to this, you also have a very considerate nature. At the same time, you are prone to overthinking and losing yourself. A medium line stretches up to the ring finger. Most people have this kind of headline. It indicates that you are smart, intelligent, and brilliant, sometimes more than those with a longer headline. A short headline stops under the middle finger. In this case, it portrays that you are hasty, careless, indecisive, and impulsive. It may also mean you are slow to respond. But the pro is that you are also very strategic.

- **Straight**: A straight headline means you are intensely analytical. You are also practical and dedicated to your work. You perform well in Mathematics, Science, Commerce, and Technology fields.

* **Curved:** If you have a curved headline, it means you are realistic, gentle, and tolerant with powerful interpersonal skills. You tend to do well in Media, Psychology, Literature, and Social Sciences fields.

* **Steeped:** If your headline steeps downward, it means you use your imagination a lot. It also points to creative and artistic abilities. Also, you may be prone to emotional influence. You also have a tendency to spend money lavishly when you are in a bad mood.

Markings that often appear with the headline include:

* **Branches:** If a downward branch appears at the end of your headline, it suggests that you are good at analyzing and solving problems through critical thinking. The longer the branch, the healthier you are at thinking and analyzing. An upward branch suggests an ability to adapt to any social environment. It also means you are good at handling business. If the branch extends beneath your ring finger, it means you have great talents, and you could be outstanding in art. A branch that extends up to the Mount of Jupiter means you want wealth, fame, and power.

* **Tassels:** If you have tassels at the end of your headline, it is a hint you may get a headache due to low blood pressure. And it could be an indicator of a weak heart. Because of this, you need to do cardio exercises to safeguard yourself against looming heart diseases.

* **Island:** An island on your headline means you are distracted and frustrated with your memory. The bigger the island, the more serious your memory problem is. The location of the island could also change its meaning. If you observe an island beneath your Mount of Jupiter, it indicates you have a nutrition problem. It also means an inability to concentrate. If the island is below the Mount of Saturn, you

are prone to depression and headaches. Also, you may suffer from stomach problems. An island beneath the Mount of Apollo means you have a weak vision. Double islands mean you may suffer a memory decline.

• **Stars:** A star on the headline indicates that you need to protect your head to avoid having a head injury. If the star is beside the headline, it highlights your wisdom.

• **Crosses:** Crossings on your headline signify timidity and cowardice. You are prone to anxiety and fear. Again, it also means you should protect your head from injury or accidents. Three crossings on your headline could be an indication of coronary disease.

• **Chains**: A chained headline is quite common among people. It suggests a lack of concentration and fluctuating attention. If the chains are at the head line's start, you may have problems involving poor memory and distorted thoughts while, if the chain appears throughout the headline, you may be prone to brain problems. You may also be mentally weak.

• **Broken:** A broken headline suggests that you will suffer from an unexpected illness. If the line breaks intermittently, it means you can't live harmoniously with a romantic partner. You always end up breaking things off. A broken headline could also suggest an interruption in the progress of your career.

As I mentioned earlier, when the headline meets the heart line, it is called the Simian Line. The Simian Line indicates an ability to create wealth and succeed. Here is an image of the simian crease.

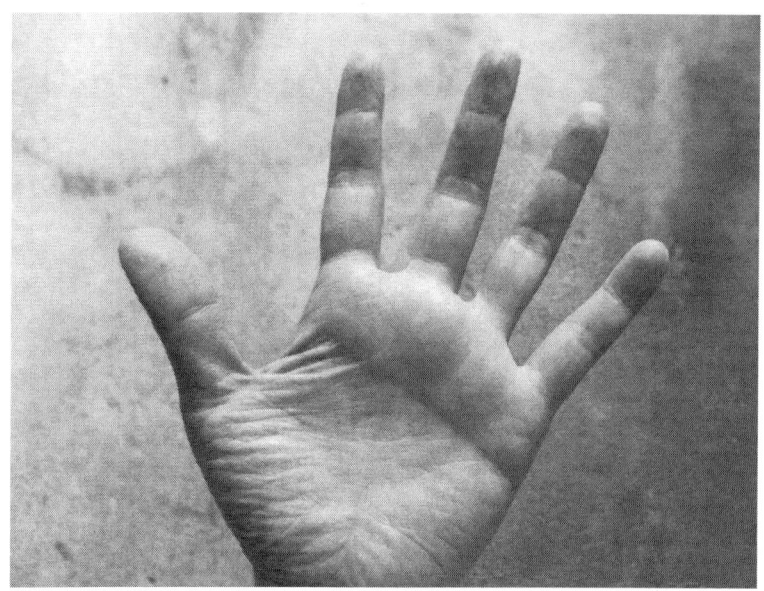

Simian Line on Left Hand

Besides the three major lines, you should also know how to read the fate line and the marriage line. So, below is a brief explanation of both.

Fate Line

Description: The fate line extends vertically from the palm's base towards the base of the middle finger. Sometimes, it may begin from the middle of the palm.

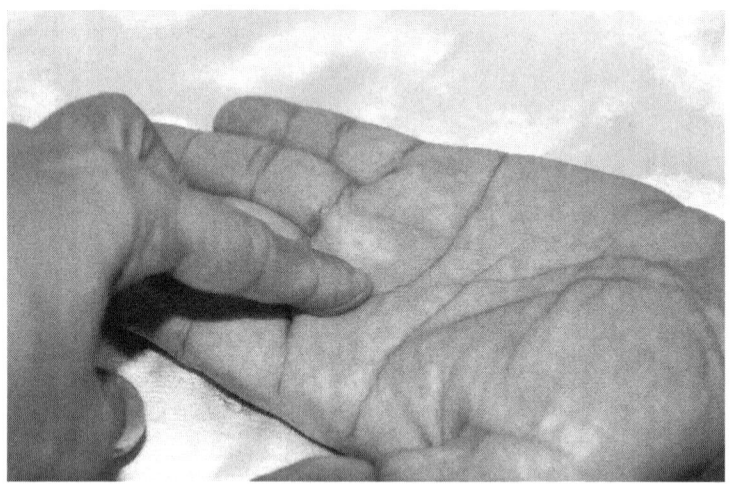

The fate line is also a significant line on the hand. It points up to the Saturn finger, so it is also called the Saturn line. In Chinese palmistry, the fate line is also considered the career line. This is because it mainly reveals information about one's career and career changes over a lifetime. A typically good fate line is clear, deep, and straight with minimal crosses. If you have this fate line, that means you have a good fortune career-wise.

Some also call it the Luck line since it mostly reflects luck and success. Some people don't have the fate line on their palms. The absence of a fate line on the palm does not mean you won't have a career. It just means you don't have a permanent career because you are always changing. This could be caused by an abundance of versatility or carelessness, depending on other factors. Or maybe you never find work you have an interest in.

The fate line can be deep and long. This line goes from the base of your palm to the point under your middle finger, your Saturn finger. A deep and long fate line suggests an innate ability to run your own business. It also shows you place much importance on credibility. Thus, you run a successful business regardless of endless challenges. Suppose the line becomes thinner and narrower from the middle of the palm. There, it suggests a smooth career at your younger age and harsh fortune as you get older, particularly after middle age.

A shallow fate line means you are a hard worker, and your career will be full of twists and turns. If the line is wide and shallow, it means you may not accomplish great things despite working hard. A shallow and narrow line suggests you are not the type to be held down by a common destiny.

An oblique fate line indicates an ability to develop unique ideas that can push your career further up. You are good at finding shortcuts to success in your career.

The location of your fate line on the palm can make all the difference.

- **Begins from the Lifeline**: If your fate line starts from your lifeline, it means you are full of energy and high vitality. It also means that your social status will be upgraded if you keep working hard. Even though you may not accomplish great things in life, you are bound to live a good and fulfilled life.

- **Begins from the Headline**: If the fate line joins with your headline at the beginning, it means that your achievements may not begin until you are above 35 years. Before 35, there will be a lot of challenges and obstructions on your way to success. Your fortune will experience a swift change after you clock 35. With your wisdom and experience, you can achieve great things.

- **Begins from the Heart Line:** A fate line linked to the heart line at the beginning indicates late success. You may not find stability in your career and life until you are well over your youth. After you pass the 50-year mark, you will likely start enjoying good fortune while working hard.

Marriage Line

Description: The marriage line is below the root of your little finger, a little above the heart line.

The marriage line is often called the relationship line. Although it is relationship and affection, the marriage line differs from the love line. Some people have one marriage line, while some have multiple. Some have no marriage line at all. The longest marriage line is typically used for analysis for people with multiple marriage lines.

A straight and long marriage line symbolized deep love; it means you are a passionate and gentle person and will end up with a happy family. A marriage line that is deep and long means you will enjoy a happy and lasting marriage. More importantly, you will also achieve success in your career even after marriage.

A short marriage line indicates a lack of passion for relationships. If the line is also shallow, you don't have enough patience to build a romantic relationship with another person. It also connotes that you find it hard to fall deeply in love. If you have this kind of line, you will likely get married late.

If your marriage line is curved, it can go two ways. A downward curve means that your partner may depart before you, likely due to an accident. If it touches your heart line, it means you will experience marital crises and dispute, after which a separation may happen. If the marriage line curves upward, it means you will have a stable and settled marriage. You may also be lucky to get married to an extremely wealthy partner. Your marriage will be happy and coordinated.

A forked marriage line indicates separation or divorce, especially if the fork looks like the letter "Y." If the fork isn't big, the separation will only be for a short while, after which there will be a reunion and a happy-ever-after. If the fork has split ends, it means you will experience marital disputes and significant crises. Your whole marriage may be one big source of confusion and frustration for you.

A broken marriage line means you are prone to setbacks in your marriage and relationships. The longer the interval between the broken parts, the more setbacks you will experience in marriage. If the break is short, you may make up with your partner.

Islands on the marriage line mean you are mentally incompatible with your partner. It is also an indicator of family conflicts. Suppose the island is at the beginning of your marriage line. There, you may not have a smooth love relationship or marriage. In the middle, it means you will experience twists and turns on your way to marriage. At the end of the line, it indicates challenges and obstacles after marriage. Multiple islands indicate that marriage may be unfavorable for you.

What do the numbers of marriage lines mean?

An absence of a marriage line means you don't desire to love or marry. You want to focus on yourself without paying attention to anybody else. If you are still below 20, your marriage line may still be developing. If you are married and don't have that line, you are only tolerating the marriage.

A single marriage line means you will fall in love, get married, and live a happy life with the ideal person. If the line is long enough, you will have a lasting and healthy marriage.

More than one marriage line may mean different things. Most people assume that it means one will get married more than once, but this is not right. Two marriage lines could mean you will separate from a partner and reunite again. Three marriage lines mean you have mixed emotions about your marriage. Marriages lines are sometimes up to six in some people. The more the lines, the more complicated their marriage will be.

Conclusion

Now, you know how you can unlock the art of palm reading to learn more about yourself and your future. This book has provided a great deal of information on how you can read your hands to discover what lies ahead for you in your career, relationship, health, and other vital aspects of your life. The next step is to start putting everything you've learned into practice to make a difference in your life. Good luck!

Here's another book by Mari Silva that you might like

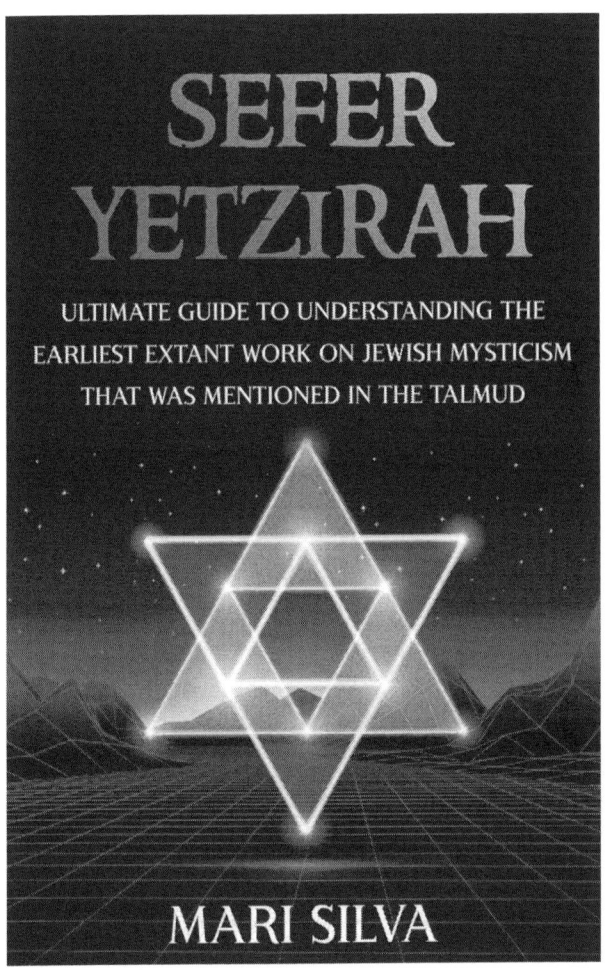

Your Free Gift (only available for a limited time)

Thanks for getting this book! If you want to learn more about various spirituality topics, then join Mari Silva's community and get a free guided meditation MP3 for awakening your third eye. This guided meditation mp3 is designed to open and strengthen ones third eye so you can experience a higher state of consciousness. Simply visit the link below the image to get started.

https://spiritualityspot.com/meditation

References

Best Palmistry Institute in Delhi, Renowned Palmist Astrologer, Best Palmistry Online | Institute of Palmistry. (n.d.). Www.Instituteofpalmistry.com. Retrieved from https://www.instituteofpalmistry.com/

Palmistry- Mounts guide for PALM READING - Palmistry online. (n.d.). Palmistry.Findyourfate.com. Retrieved from https://palmistry.findyourfate.com/palmistry-mounts.htm

(PDF) A Novel Approach for Hand Analysis Using Image Processing Techniques. (n.d.). ResearchGate. Retrieved from https://www.researchgate.net/publication/44288389_A_Novel_Approach_for_Hand_Analysis_Using_Image_Processing_Techniques

Scientific Palmistry - What Science Can Tell About Us from Our Hands - Blifaloo.com. (n.d.). Retrieved from http://www.blifaloo.com/palm-reading/

Space/Gaps between Fingers Meaning in Palmistry. (n.d.). Your Chinese Astrology. Retrieved from https://www.yourchineseastrology.com/palmistry/finger/space-between-fingers.htm

The Art and Science of Hand Reading: Classical Methods for Self-Discovery through Palmistry - Kindle edition by Goldberg, Ellen, Bergen, Dorian. Religion & Spirituality Kindle eBooks @ Amazon.com. (2020). Amazon.com. https://www.amazon.com/Art-Science-Hand-Reading-Self-Discovery-ebook/dp/B01BX0WBSO/ref=tmm_kin_swatch_0?_encoding=UTF8&qid=1601267320&sr=8-2

Ward, K. (2019, November 12). The Beginner's Guide to Palm Reading. Cosmopolitan. https://www.cosmopolitan.com/lifestyle/a29623751/how-to-read-palms-b

Printed in Great Britain
by Amazon